AURANGABAD
JEWEL OF THE DECCAN

RASHMI JOLLY

NIYOGI BOOKS

Published by
NIYOGI BOOKS
Block D, Building No. 77,
Okhla Industrial Area, Phase-I,
New Delhi-110 020, INDIA
Tel: 91-11-26816301, 26818960
Email: niyogibooks@gmail.com
Website: www.niyogibooksindia.com

Text and images © Rashmi Jolly
Photographs of Ajanta © Binoy K Behl
Image on page 11 © Dr Rafat Qureshi & Dr Dulari Qureshi

Design: Shaju K Anthony

ISBN: 978-93-91125-59-2
Publication: 2022

Printed at: Niyogi Offset Pvt. Ltd., New Delhi, India

*Dedicated to the ancient city of Aurangabad
and its ancient architecture, art and culture.*

CONTENTS

PREFACE

I have travelled regularly to Aurangabad from 1976 and have seen it grow from a sleepy little town to a big, bustling, industrial city today. I have felt very strongly that, even though the most beautiful books and pictures have been produced on the ancient art, history and culture of Aurangabad, it still remains an area less known and less travelled.

I saw, I read and I researched. My humble endeavour was to gather not just historical and cultural information which the best and brightest minds have covered extensively in the past, but also to try and write a sufficiently accurate, useful, practical and simple guide to lure travellers to what I consider the 'Jewel of the Deccan'. However, at the time of going to the press, some things may have changed in Aurangabad. Good places may have become bad and bad places may have become better! Any such omission or oversight on my part may please be forgiven.

Please note that the discerning reader may come across an occasional slight difference either in the spelling of certain words or dates. These variations occur as they represent references taken from differing opinions. All are given credit in the bibliography.

As I still continue to be a person belonging to the old order, I find I am not so adept and computer savvy as I should be in keeping with the times. Everything I wrote, corrected and rewrote was painstakingly done in long hand. The task was sometimes daunting, however, I persisted and persevered.

Rashmi A. Jolly

INTRODUCTION

HISTORICAL BACKGROUND

Every foreign tourist travelling to India is lured towards the 'golden triangle' of Delhi, Agra and Jaipur. Many get to Goa and as far as Kerala, but how many of them know of the hidden jewel that is Aurangabad? Of the over 721 sites on the World Heritage List of 2001 compiled by UNESCO, some eighteen sites have been identified in India so far. Of these, the Ajanta and Ellora caves at Aurangabad were listed in 1983.

Some 1500 years before Christ assimilated all his ideas and men, this synthetic genius of India had the capacity to amalgamate and fuse many religions. It resisted and yet, simultaneously absorbed and coalesced with foreign cultures. The history of India is not the story of how she underwent foreign invasions, but how she resisted them and eventually, somehow triumphed over them.

Successive cultural influences have fused together to form this fascinating country called India. Layers of diverse elements have produced a cohesive society with a unique social fabric. This synthesizing process flowered into a varied civilization during five millennia which saw the development of great creeds: Hinduism, Buddhism, Jainism and later, Islam, followed by Sikhism.

Historic India is not merely a country, but a culture based on a solid foundation transmuted from several beginnings which unifies the diversity that is India.

The early ancient history of Aurangabad is somewhat of a mystery, and scholars have often remarked that during its early period, India lacked a Western sense of history as no accurate records were kept. India always had a tradition of oral narration, which was passed down from generation to generation, either through legendary stories, ballad poetry or drama.

The first historical reference to Aurangabad is found in the Kanheri inscriptions of the Kanheri Chaitya Cave No. 4, dating to 2nd century B.C. In a brief survey of the history of Aurangabad, the earliest available reference is to the Satavahana dynasty around 220 B.C. The next dynasty to dominate Aurangabad was the Vakatakas in about 250 A.D. They ruled for some 300 years. The Chalukyas hold dominion over an extensive region of the Deccan from about the middle of the 6th century to about the 8th century A.D. They were followed by the Rashtrakutas, whose rule lasted from 748 to 973 A.D. The last Hindu dynasty to rule this region was the Yadava around 1069 A.D. After 1271 A.D., Muslim rulers of the Sultanate of Delhi began raiding the Deccan. They were later followed by the Mughals.

In the late 16th and early 17th century, several nobles and generals of Abyssinian origin rose to fame in the complex and shifting web of Sultanates in the Deccan Peninsula. They offered strong resistance to the Mughals.

Malik Ambar was one of the Abyssinians or 'Habshi' known for his dynamism, and he was a staunch enemy of the imperial Mughal hegemony. Malik Ambar was born around 1549 and as a child was sold to a Baghdadi slave trader heading for the Deccan. Following a civil war in 1596, he allied himself with another Abyssinian, Abhang Khan, in an uprising against Queen Chand Bibi. He was appointed 'Peshwa' to the Kingdom of Ahmednagar and he continued to play a key role in the resistance of the Deccan against the Mughals. For this task he received help from the Mahrattas whose power, it may be said, he was the first to develop, and it was under his banner that Shahji, the father of Shivaji laid the foundation of Mahratta greatness. Malik Ambar was not only a great general but also a statesman. His name stands out prominently in the history of the district. The revenue settlement which he perfected celebrates his name as the 'Todar Mal of the Deccan".

Malik Ambar recovered disputed territories from the Mughals and thwarted their attempts in their expansionist policies in the Deccan by keeping them at bay. In 1610 Malik Ambar, the Wazir of Murtaza, the Nizam of Ahmednagar, founded within the

औरंगाबाद-नामा

डॉ. रफत कुरेशी / डॉ. दुलारी कुरेशी

barren, grey, rocky terrain of the Deccan plateau, the city of 'Khadki' or 'Khirki' meaning 'window' implying it was the 'window of the Deccan'. He then established his capital there. Initially, it was named 'Fatehpura' or the city of victory, probably after the name of Malik Ambar's son, Fateh Khan.

Malik Ambar erected a number of palaces, mosques and public buildings. He had mountain streams dammed up near their sources to form reservoirs. Under his orders, the Moti Talao at Jalna was constructed and the water supply system was connected to it. Aurangabad receives its water supply from springs and wells connected with small underground masonry pipes. The principal water sources are fourteen in number and the most important is the canal built by Malik Ambar from the river near Harsul. This formidable Peshwa died in 1626 and it was only during Aurangzeb's rule that the Mughals progressively annexed the Deccan Sultanates.

Aurangzeb was sent to Khirki as the Governor of the Deccan in 1634 and the city became his residence. In 1681 Aurangzeb became the Mughal Emperor. This city went on to become historically famous under its present name 'Aurangabad'—it is a Persian word meaning 'Built by the Throne' and is named after the Mughal emperor, Aurangzeb.

Aurangzeb, a Persian word meaning the 'Throne's Ornament', ascended his father's throne by usurping it. He imprisoned his father, Emperor Shah Jehan, beheaded his eldest brother Dara Shikoh and later his youngest brother. On ascending the throne Aurangzeb took the title of 'Alamgir' or 'Conqueror of the World'. An argument he often used to support his action in deposing his father and seizing the throne was that he believed he was more competent than Shah Jehan!

Aurangzeb's predecessors had built up for themselves a permanent place in history. He too had similar ambitions. According to Rekha Joshi, his objectives were three-fold: expansion of Mughal Empire, consolidation of Mughal Empire and protection of Mughal Empire. Aurangzeb formulated his policies in keeping with his adopted title of 'Alamgir' or 'conqueror'. Sir Jadunath Sarkar in his five volumes on Aurangzeb gives minute details of the life and times of Aurangzeb. The learned historian points out that 'Aurangzeb wanted to revitalize the forces of Islam in order to establish "Darul-Islam". Aurangzeb wanted to be a great and successful ruler, a fine statesman, a clever politician and a mighty conqueror.'

Aurangzeb adopted a vigorous military policy. As an emperor and an educated man he travelled around tirelessly, sleeping and living in rough conditions in military camps. Aurangzeb had a complex personality and in fact, he was a bundle of contradictions. As an emperor he was both austere and accessible, mean and merciful, cruel and kind, generous and selfish, and always changeable. He has been presented as an intellectual and a lover of all things Islamic, as well as a military man of action.

During his reign, well-known European travelers like Tavernier and François Bernier travelled the length and breadth of the Mughal empire. We have accounts of how Tavernier was invited to see Aurangzeb's exotic array of jewels and treasures.

In this collection was a drop-shaped, crystal clear, brilliant pink diamond the 'Nur-ul-Ain' or 'Light of the Eye' shown as one of the 'Great Table Diamonds'. It formed part of the loot, plundered in 1739 by Nadir Shah and taken away to Iran. Much later in history, at the wedding of Empress Farah Diba to the Shah of Iran, the Nur-ul-Ain was set in her wedding tiara by the famous jeweller Harry Winston. The European traveler Bernier was awestruck by Aurangzeb's 'Kalgi' or 'Turban Ornament', the base of which was composed of diamonds of an extraordinary size and unparallel value.

In his later years, Aurangzeb is seen as a man in 'antiquity' wearing a grey beard symbolizing him as a philosopher or a wise man with an inquisitive mind. It is almost as though a softer side has now emerged from his earlier hard and autocratic ways. The everlasting fame of the Mughals was fabled with immense aura and glory in the West. Pride of place goes in huge measure to their architectural achievements. The last of the Great Mughals, Emperor Aurangzeb, left an indelible mark in the Deccan Peninsula.

Architecture is visual art. The Muslim architecture of Aurangabad lies firmly in the Deccan tradition—from the oldest structures of the early 14th century to the later architecture which developed its own local stylistic characteristics at Aurangabad.

According to Vidya Dehejia, 'The Deccani style of art originated from two different strands. One derived from local craftsmen and the second from the foreign Islamic population of the Deccan which included Turks, Persians, Arabs and Africans. Skilled craftsmen, who arrived from the Persian Gulf in Arab ships that docked at the ports along the west coast of India, contributed towards the novel aesthetic sense seen in the arts of the Deccan'.

Artists as we know are 'born to create'; it's their only 'raison d'etre'. Rich styles and varied and intricate forms of the Jains of Gujarat were borrowed and innovatively adapted for Islamic ends. There is no end to the fabulousness, and the result is a fascinating architectural style. By implication, the architecture of Aurangabad is a sheer 'tour de force'.

GEOGRAPHICAL FEATURES

The district of Aurangabad occupies an area of approximately 10,107 sq.km. In its physical features, it is divided into two distinct sections consisting of the 'uplands' to the north, and the 'lowlands' to the south. The low country is exceedingly fertile and cultivated. The view of these plains is monotonous and destitute of trees which can only be seen here and there in scattered clumps marking village sites.

The elevated region or uplands cannot be referred to as hills as they are really a series of flat-topped plateaus. Here too, the general character of the vegetation is marked by the prevalence of tall grass and a paucity of huge trees.

FLORA AND FAUNA

Throughout its history, Aurangabad has long been famous for providing hunting grounds, especially for British officers. 'The banks of the River Godavari were at one time famous for the breed of horses known as the "Dakhani". These horses were notorious for their hardiness and endurance powers. A hundred years ago, Mahratta horsemen scoured the Indian country side astride these. The Dakhani breed of horses is said to have sprung from the cross-breeding of the country mare with the Arab horse. Even today, the remarkable "Dakhan horse" inherited many of the excellent qualities of his noble progenitor and breeding establishments which still exist'. Other animals of Aurangabad district are the domestic ones, namely: cows, bullocks, goats, sheep and asses. They graze and feed on the fields of tall grass.

CITY

Aurangabad, a city in Maharashtra, in Western India, lies along the Khan river in the Dudhana Valley between the Lakenvara hills to the north and the Satara hill range to the south. Aurangabad lies at an altitude of 513 meters or 1,683 ft. The total district area is 10,100 sq.km, of which the urban area is 141.1 sq.km and 99,587 sq.km is rural. According to the census of 2011, the population figure is 3,701,282.

CLIMATE

Annual temperature in Aurangabad range from 9° to 40°C. The lowest recorded temperature was 2°C and the highest 46°C. The average annual rainfall which occurs during the monsoon season from June to September is 727 mm. The best time to visit Aurangabad is during the winter i.e. from October to February end, when temperature can range from approximately 18°C down to about 12°C.

WALLED CITY

Aurangabad is referred to as a walled city. This wall is an extraordinary relic. It was built in 1682 by Aurangzeb to protect the city from the incursions and sporadic attacks of the Marathas. The long, low, stub of the rampart is snaked around over uneven lines of crags like the articulated tail of a stone lizard. What had once probably been a fortified wall of not a great height, approximately 14 ft high in most places with small turrets and terraces, is now reduced to a few courses of fine-hewn stones topped with ragged turf. 'The wall is of solid masonry. The battlements are loop-holed for musketry and the merlons over the gateways, and at certain places along the wall are machicolated. Semi-circular bastions surmounted by towers, occur at each flanking angle and at regular intervals. The wall is pierced by thirteen gateways and its total length is over six miles'. Its appeal lies in the sheer scale of the wall and in its hugeness. Over the centuries, the wall has seemingly fused into the landscape and this feat of engineering has become a geological feature. Why was this wall built? A wall's role is one of fortification, interpreting it as a symbolic frontier-marker of protection. What is the complex political psychology behind frontier lines such as this one? Walls are not built simply to keep people out; they can keep people in as we have seen with the 'Ghetto' wall in Warsaw, Poland.

Most important of all, construction on this scale was also a spectacular and permanent demonstration of the power and efficiency of an empire. Its propaganda value nearly 350 years ago would have been immense. No doubt, kings and emperors understood the power of architecture and indeed had a passion for it as did the Great Mughals. However, the Aurangabad of Aurangzeb's time was not all included within city walls, as ancient suburbs can be traced which have since disappeared. When Aurangzeb made Aurangabad his capital, he added 54 suburbs which were walled in the city itself.

For military reasons, a wall like this also holds the best vantage points. Hence you also get the best views. In its heady mix of ruins and greenery, this wall remains an inspiration and impressive even today.

GATES OR DARWAZAS

There are 52 gates and barring only one (Bhadkal Gate), all the others are associated with the period of Aurangzeb. The main gates face the four directions: Delhi gate to the North, Paithan gate to the South, Mecca or Makai gate to the East and Jalna or Khas gate to the West.

All the gates were built of limestone and even bricks. In old building methods, wrought iron was used for strengthening joints whereas today, it would be steel. Gates acted as watch-posts. Some names of the gates sound interesting, namely: Khooni Darwaza or Bloody Gate, Kaala Darwaza or Black Gate, Chawal Darwaza or Rice Gate, Rangeen Darwaza or Colourful Gate, Roshan Darwaza or Light Gate. Roshanara meaning 'light' was the name of Aurangzeb's sister to whom he was very attached. She remained his favourite friend and advisor.

Due to centuries of neglect, majority of the 52 gates are in ruins and today only 13 survive. Of these, only six gates survive in good condition as some restoration has taken place. On two other gates the restoration is going on. But the remaining ones are in grave danger of being lost if urgent repairs are not undertaken to preserve these as monuments. The journey from ruin to monument is often fraught with complications. 'Ruin implies decrepitude however beautiful the remains may be. "Monument" suggests heritage, something precious and worth conserving. Some financial aid has come from overseas namely, Japan. Alas! In most of our heritage monuments, often only a blue and white painted metal sign goes up'. 'This is the property of the Archaeological Survey of India!'

Delhi Gate or Delhi Darwaza

DELHI GATE OR DELHI DARWAZA IN THE NORTH

This was the largest, most stately and majestic gate built by Aurangzeb. Its architectural features namely, the pointed archway forming a portico is similar in design to Lahore Gate at Delhi's Red Fort or Lal Qila. To the right of Delhi Gate is a picturesque lake, originally known as Khizar Lake, created in Aurangzeb's reign. This grand gate is still in a fairly good state of preservation.

PAITHAN GATE OR PAITHAN DARWAZA TO THE SOUTH

This gate, though smaller in size than the historic Delhi Gate, was the royal gateway leading to Paithan. The medieval name of Paithan was 'Pratisthana' during the rule of the

Paithan Gate or Paithan Darwaza

Satavahana Dynasty and it was an important commercial centre. This old historical gate, though one of the principal gates of Aurangzeb's capital, has a simple archway and a plain ceiling. A huge wooden doorway studded with iron nails is still fairly well preserved.

MECCA GATE OR MAKAI DARWAZA TO THE WEST

This gate is located in Begumpura. It is an imposing gate and the only gate which has a cannon installed. For strategic reasons, only all the important gates had cannons.

JALNA GATE OR KHAS DARWAZA TO THE EAST

This gate still stands and architecturally is a simple structure.

Delhi Gate or Delhi Darwaza

KILA-E-ARK DARWAZA

This was the principal gate to the Quil-e-ark palace. This palace was constructed on the orders of Aurangzeb. The palace had its own fortification walls further guarded by five gates. Kila-e-ark Darwaza is a lofty gate and its silhouette reminds one of the days of pomp and glory. It is crowned by four arches in a sequel. The interior consists of rooms where perhaps the gate-keepers resided. Unfortunately, it is in a sad state of ruin and decline as trees have taken root in the main central arch. The roots have penetrated deep inside and there is a danger the structure could collapse.

Bhadkal Gate

BHADKAL GATE ALSO KNOWN AS BAHARKUL DARWAZA

This gate is one of the tallest and most imposing gates in the city. It is a symbol of the victory of Malik Ambar against the Mughals in 1612 A.D. Malik Ambar was an ingenious architect himself and had incorporated special techniques of building a ribbed vault. This style of construction was improvised over the years and is found in the Gothic architecture in Europe. The gate is built in lime and basalt rock found in the Deccan. On the first floor is the 'Naqarkhana' where 'Naubat' or music was played on special events. The first floor is reached by a flight of stairs on either side from the

Naubat Gate

outside. There are three open arches on the first floor on all four sides. This gate bears the traditional mark and design of an inverted lotus, an indication that it was built in Malik Ambar's reign. The gate is in a fairly good condition.

BIBI-KA-MAQBARA

The tomb of Begum Rabia Durani (wife of Emperor Aurangzeb) was built by her son Prince Azam Shah in 1678. As a tribute to his beloved 'Bibi' meaning 'Mother' designed by the architect Ata Aula, the mausoleum stands beyond an area known as Begumpura in an enclosure of approximately 457 metres by 274 metres. The Tawarikh-Nama of Aurangzeb's reign, written by Ghulam Mustafa gives the figure of Rs. 6,68,203/- as the cost of construction of the mausoleum at that time. The tomb is a square building and is closely modelled on Shah Jehan's Taj Mahal.

Colourful Gate or Rangeen Darwaza

Black Gate or Kaala Darwaza

Bibi-Ka-Maqbara

However, as the Mughal empire declined by now to a state of insolvency, the opportunity for grand architectural projects had severly diminished. This rapid decline in architectural design can be seen in the comparison between the Taj Mahal, the mausoleum for Shah Jehan's 'Biwi' or 'Wife' and the tomb built for Aurangzeb's wife by her son for his 'Bibi' or 'Mother' forty years later.

Bibi-ka-Maqbara is visible for miles from a long distance on the road between Daulatabad and Aurangabad. Bibi-ka-Maqbara, though inspired by the Taj Mahal, is of half its size and a pale imitation of the greatest monument of love. Phillip Davies records: 'The proportions are compressed and the ornamental detail is clumsily

Bibi-Ka-Maqbara

executed, verging on the decadent, a sterile exercise in architectural plagiarism and a travesty of its original prototype'.

It has four slender minarets with bulbous domes which stand freely at the corners of the terrace. 'The surrounding high wall is crenellated with pointed arches recessed on the outside. There are bastions at intervals and the recesses are divided by pilaster crowned with little minarets. The centre of the southern wall is occupied by a handsome portal entrance, closed by folding doors which are covered with a running foliage pattern in brass'. The gateway doors have the architect's name inscribed.

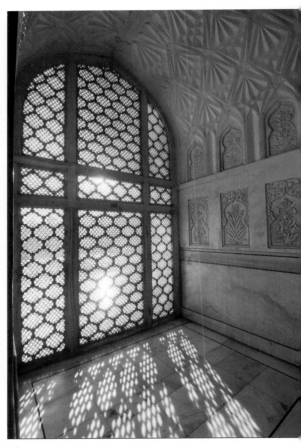

Bibi-Ka-Maqbara

The garden in front or 'Char Baug' is divided into quadrants by water courses, crossed at right angles by other channels emphasizing the role of water as the symbolic and physical source of life. The interaction of the channels of water represent the meeting of Man and God.

In early Islam, tomb-building was prohibited as glorifying a grave by constructing a building over it would run counter to the equality of all men in death. It seems ironic that a creed which began with such stringent restrictions against all forms of monumental funerary art should develop in such a way as to produce some of the most splendid examples in the world. Actually, the concept of a tomb in a walled enclosure pre dated the Mughals. Phillip Davies says, 'The word "paradise" is a transliteration of the old Persian word "Pairideaza" which means "A walled garden". The location of a monumental tomb, at the centre of an enclosed garden alluded to basic cosmological ideas. The garden was a microcosm of the physical world, organized symmetrically and axially in accordance with contemporary cosmological beliefs. At the centre lay the tomb, the material universe, crowned by a dome, the symbol of eternity.'

Bibi-ka-Maqbara is an unexpected little gem of dilapidated splendour. The weathered exterior speaks of decades of neglect from previous cenuries but its iron pillars and plaster carvings remain intact and a magical atmosphere still lingers.

Jean Baptiste Tavernier, a renowned French traveler, during the period of 17th century was in Hindoostan at the time of Shah Jehan's passing. He recorded the fact that 'Shah Jehan had intended a replica of the Taj in black marble, to be built as his own mausoleum, on the opposite bank of the Jamuna river connected with his wife's tomb by a bridge. The parsimonious Aurangzeb refused to carry out this grand design and placed his father without more ado in the existing Taj. This legend has been current ever since, although there is no other contemporary evidence to support it. The relative position of the two marble coffins is often pointed out in confirmation of Tavernier's theory namely, Mumtaz Mahal occupies the very centre directly beneath the central dome, laid out in perfect symmetry with the entrances while the Great Moghul is to one side in a slightly inferior position but raised on a plinth'.

MOSQUE

The 'Mosque' or Masjid is the principal social, political and religious centre of Islam, intended for daily prayers. It is a public place of worship where one prostrates oneself for prayer. Essentially, its form is derived from the humble house of the Prophet at Medina, an open courtyard surrounded by a colonnade of palm trunks covered with palm leaves. In India, the principal form and structure of the mosque were imported from Persia during the period of the Sultanate with 'iwans' or vaulted halls open at one end, enriched with highly decorated facades and domes.

A mosque has a courtyard, perhaps rectangular in shape with a covered prayer hall. In the centre there is usually a fountain or a tank for religious ablutions. The cloisters on the Mecca side were enlarged into a sanctuary, with a wall containing an 'alcove' or 'mihrab', very essential for indicating the 'qibla' or direction to face when saying prayers. Mosques also normally have minarets with high platforms from where the faithful can be summoned to the 'Juma' or 'Friday' prayers.

A mosque was open, functional and devoid of imagery. Walled surfaces were either plain or vividly painted with glazed surfaces enriched with decorative calligraphy from the Quran. Calligraphy was regarded as the highest of the arts. An ancient Muslim saying runs 'Good Writing makes the truth stand out'. Calligraphy, was combined with foliated decoration of classical vine and scroll designs, curling tendrils of intertwined leaves and the Hindu element of the lotus flower.

JAMA MASJID

The Jama Masjid lies near Kila Arak. It has fifty polygonal pillars arranged in five rows, connected by a series of arches which create twenty-seven equal compartments, each covered by a domed vault. There are nine pointed arches to the front, five of which were constructed by Malik Ambar in 1612, the remaining four by Aurangzeb. The cornice is bracketed and the parapet above is perforated. The corner angles have octagonal shafts, ornamented with discs carrying little domes. The quadrangle has accommodation for travelers on three sides and a cistern at the centre.

KALI MASJID

In 1600 A.D., Malik Ambar built seven stone mosques. The earliest was built in Juna Bazaar and is a six-pillared stone building on a high plinth. There are other mosques located at Begumpura, Shah Bazaar, Nawabpura Chowk, Jama Masjid, etc. They are known by the general term 'Kali Masjid'. The construction material used are black rock cubes, hence the name.

SHAH GANJ MASJID

In the great market square is this large masjid, built in about 1720 A.D. It is on a raised platform with shops on three sides, the fourth being open, and a flight of steps which leads to an open arcade of five scalloped arches constructed in the Indo-Saracenic style of architecture supported on stone pillars. The interior has twenty-four pillars, the main portion is crowned by a bulbous dome and elegant spire, with a base adorned with carved lotus leaves tied in a neat narrow band.

The east and west wings form arcaded monasteries or chambers called Kham Khas and consists of five arches on either side. There are minarets at the corners of the main building and also at the end angles of the Kham Khas. The courtyard entrance in front is in the shape of a little mosque with a pointed arch and two minarets. The courtyard also contains two large cisterns.

CHAUK MASJID

This was built in 1665 by Shaysista Khan, the maternal uncle of Aurangzeb. It has a front of five pointed arches carved in depth. There are eight pillars supporting five onion domes and the central dome is lofty with a metallic spire. Similar to the Shah Ganj Masjid, there are shops at the base of the raised platform and a gateway with two minarets.

Pan Chakki

LAL MASJID

This Masjid was built in 1655 by Zainu-ul-Abidin-Mufti, the superintendent of buildings in Aurangzeb's time. It is in red-painted basalt enriched with stucco.

DARGAH

A 'Dargah' is a Persian word actually meaning a 'court' or a 'palace'. However, dargahs are really holy shrines or places of pilgrimage and contain the remains of Sufi Saints. In a dargah, the grave will have the body suitably placed with the head to the north, lying on the right hand-side with the face towards Mecca. Great importance is attached to the psychic or spiritual energy emanating from the graves of such holy men.

DARGAH OF BABA SHAHMUZAFFAR

This dargah is situated on the road from the cantonment to Begumpura Bridge. Baba Shah, who died in 1687 A.D., was the spiritual guru or guide of Aurangzeb and is buried here. The dargah has a mosque, a madrassa, a kachari, a sarai and zenanas. The place is famous for housing a very big library of rare Persian and Arabic books and manuscripts.

The tomb itself is a plain edifice of red porphyry surrounded by a screen of cusped arches on stone pillars. The outer buildings are designed in similar styles with projecting kiosks crowned by the bent style of Bengali roofs. There are several masonry tanks, numerous fountains and a larger cistern in front with a water mill for grinding corn. The water mill is known as 'Panchakki'.

MAUSOLEUM OF PIR ISMAIL

Outside Delhi Gate on Harsul road, built in the late 17th century is this mausoleum of a famous tutor of Aurangzeb. The archiecture is a combination of Mughal and Pathan themes. The entrance gate has a high pointed Pathan style archway and each corner of the terrace has a little tower capped by a Moghul style bulbous, onion dome and final.

PAN CHAKKI

This water mill for grinding corn was erected in 1695 and is surrounded by other buildings. These buildings were constructed by a noble on the staff of Chin Kalich Khan. An oblong reservoir was added in about 1715 by Jamil Beg Khan. The water mill is fed by an underground conduit via the Pan Chakki reservoir. The cistern in front of the mosque forms the roof of a large hall beneath on massive pillars. The Pan Chakki area forms one of the picturesque parts of Aurangabad city. The Kaula Nala skirts around the garden and has a bridge with pointed arches going over it followed by a second bridge lower down. The walls of Begumpura are to the right and the city walls are to the left.

In the south-west corner of the mosque is the tomb or 'dargah' of Burhanud-din-at-Roza. It is very plain and on a platform of porphyry. There is some perforated white marble work in the front and the tombs of Aurangzeb's son Azam Shah and his wife and daughter are also close by. The floor is of white marble and a neat perforated marble railing is on three sides. The crowning glory of Pan Chakki is not just the architectural beauty of all its buildings, but it's most advanced and excellent water system whereby the inhabitants procured the sweetest water to drink. But alas! Water has now become so scarce!

DAULATABAD FORT

'Daulatabad' or the 'city of fortune' is a famous and formidable hill-fort very close to the Ellora caves. It is situated 9 miles north-west of Aurangabad. It is famous as the old Hindu capital of Deogiri and it was the gateway to the city. Deogiri was the capital of the Raja of the Yadava Dynasty and this fort was first captured by Alauddin Khilji in 1296. The Raja eventually got the fort back but subsequent invasions and occupations of different rules followed in 1318, the last Raja Harpad was flayed alive. The fort became an important centre for Muslim operations and Ghiyath-ud-Din Muhammad Tughlak II made it his capital by transferring the entire population of Delhi to Deogiri, renaming it as Daulatabad. However, the venture was a disastrous failure. The forced wholesale migration of the entire Muslim population from Delhi to the Deccan was defeated by acute famine and scarcity of water. The people were compelled to return.

Nevertheless, as a result of this mass movement of people, the roots of Muslim culture and architecture were planted in the Deccan. The Daulatabad Fort stayed in the possession of the Bahmani's until 1526 when it finally came into the hands of the Mughal ruler Shah Jehan. It remained under Mughal control until Aurangzeb's death.

Daulatabad Fort

The fortress is spectacular and as Phillip Davies describes it, 'stands on a huge conical granite outcrop which rises 600 ft. the lower end about 150 ft. comprising a perpendicular scarp. There are three concentric lines of fortification between the outer wall and the citadel. The outer walls, which are entered via three gateways, enclose the original town of Deogiri, of which little remains'.

In 1318, during the rule of Qutbuddin Khilji, the Jama Masjid was built in Daulatabad. It was originally a Jain temple that eventually got converted into a mosque. It is a large enclosed square with a prayer hall consisting of 106 pillars forming 25 aisles, each five bays deep, supporting a flat roof. Four external columns carry a corbelled dome over the alcove or 'mihrab'. The architectural style of the columns show Hindu and Jain influence.

Daulatabad Fort

On the opposite side to Jama Masjid is Chand Minar built in 1435. This is an elegant 'pillar of victory' consisting of four well balanced circular storeys, with a central fluted section, erected by Alauddin Bahmani to commemorate his conquest of the fort. The base of this well preserved minaret contains twenty-four small chambers and a rather small mosque. The carved brackets of the balcony are of Hindu origin.

A third gateway, beyond the outer moat marks the entrance to inner defences. To the right of the gateway is a huge bastion protecting the gate and the drawbridge. The gate is studded with iron spikes. To the right of this third gate are the ruins of Chini Mahal or China Palace where in 1687 Aurangzeb, locked up and kept Tana Shah, the last Golconda King imprisoned for thirteen years. Still visible in the ruins of Chini

Daulatabad Fort

Mahal are some beautiful blue and yellow enamel tiles inlay. Immediately above the Chini Mahal is a circular bastion, Kila Shikan or Fort breaker, carrying a heavy piece of ordnance 22 ft long.

Phillip Davies further records, 'The moat around the citadel is crossed by a stone bridge, the level of water in the moat being controlled by dams which could render the bridge inaccessible during a siege. The way into the citadel is past a defensive tower and through a series of underground chambers and passages hewn from solid rock'.

There is a huge, monumental doorway which resembles the doorway to the Kailash Temple at Ellora. Enemy advance through the tunnel could be impeded by a stone barrier drawn on from a socket by iron rings.

Daulatabad Fort

At the head of the tunnel is a ribbed iron door, 20 ft. long and one inch thick which could be heated, burning red hot, from a small chamber in an emergency. The resulting air currents caused smoke to circulate upwards through the tunnel in order to suffocate the enemy. At the end of the tunnel is a wide flight of steps, past the Shrine of Fakir Sukh Sultan, to the Hindu Pavillion with a vernandah above a 100 ft. chasm. It is believed, to have been the residence of the Yadavi Rani of Deogiri and later was occupied by Shah Jehan. The citadel lies above, approached by a further zig-zag flight of steps and defended by two more gateways. At the summit in the west corner is a single gun about 19 ½ ft. long. On another adjacent bastion is another large cannon called Creator of Storms inscribed in Gujarati.

Daulatabad Fort

The European traveler Tavernier visited Daulatabad and there are historical records on the excellent pieces of cannon and the cannoniers who were generally English or Dutch. There was a Dutch engineer and a company from Holland involved. M. Thevenot recorded how Daulatabad was a place of great trade and commerce.

The architecture and impregnable defences of Daulatabad show rather pronounced similarities with contemporary castles in the Levant or lands, bordering the eastern shores of the Mediterranean and the Aegean seas, especially Syria and Lebanon. This proves that the Bahamani builders of Daulatabad were well acquainted with western methods of building forts and fortification.

QUILA-E-ARAK

The name means a 'citadel'. This vast complex was built in 1692 by Aurangzeb stretching between the entire area of Delhi and Mecca Gates of the city, however, now it is mostly in ruins. It consists of battlemented walls, four entrances and a 'Naqarkhana' for musicians. A high terrace to the right of the entrance still survives with an extensive garden and ruined tanks. The Am Khas, or Durbar Hall and the Jama Masjid remain intact and are of great interest. An inscription can be seen over the enclosure close to the mosque dating it to 1659.

At present this huge palace and its grounds are used by the Government College of Arts. The building is in a poor state and near to collapse making it dangerous for the students.

CHITA KHANA or PANDIT KHANA

This is a circular building with a number of rooms around a central open courtyard. It was built by Malik Ambar around the 17th century. It was for the use of learned men or pandits of Aurangabad city. However, Aurangzeb converted it into a lodge for travelers or Mahi Baz Khana. During the Nizam period it was used as Chori Mahal or the city jail. It is a circular building with a number of rooms all opening in to a courtyard.

BAARA DARI

Baara Dari at Aurangabad and Damri Mahal are adjoining buildings to Delhi gate which are now used as Kacheri's and the Collectors Office. Hardly anything of its former beauty or grandeur remains today. At the entrance are four arched doorways. The chattri windows projecting outwards are supported by lean and delicate pillars. A covered aqueduct passes over one of the buildings and in the past descended in a shower into an oblong cistern below which were many fountains.

DAMRI MAHAL

After completion of Baara Dari, the Damri Mahal was built. It derived its name from its construction which levied a contribution of a 'Damri' or a quarter of a dub, on all labourers employed at Baara Dari. An arcaded verandah projects in front like a portico and contains five scalloped arches. Behind this are 10 rooms of different sizes, arranged in a line and to the right are seven chambers with antechambers. The entrance is to the far right corner. On a slightly higher level, close by, is another small building detached from this. The roof is arched and there are two cisterns, one in front of the verandah and the other outside the building.

SONHERI MAHAL

This palace is situated in Paharsingpura, a suburb of Aurangabad, in an area with a picturesque backdrop of mountains. The entrance of the palace is dominated by a massive and impressive gateway. It was known as Sonheri Mahal or Golden Palace because of the paintings made of gold which once decorated it. The palace is constructed in stone and lime on a high plinth level. It was constructed between about 1657 and 1663 by a Raja of Bundelkhand who accompanied Aurangzeb to the Deccan. The area around Paharsingpura was known as Hanuman Tekdi or mound. There is also a memorial of Gogapir. Other famous saints like Nipat Niranjan also came here for meditation and contemplation.

NAWKHANDA PALACE

This palace was originally built by Malik Ambar. A number of buildings were added to it during the Nizam's period by Asif Jah I namely: five Zenanas, a Diwan-i-am, a Diwan-i-khas, a Masjid, a Kacheri, a garden and a cistern. The entire palace is in a dilapidated state and in ruins.

CHHATRIS

The cenotaphs of the Rajputs are called chhatris, initially borrowed from the Muslims. They are a blend of Muslim and Hindu architecture, supported on columns with lofty stylobates and octagonal domes. There are several Hindu cenotaphs, especially near the cantonment of Aurangabad but all of them are not of great importance.

The most important chhatri was built by Raja Jai Singh at Harsul, near Aurangabad. This chhatri consisted of an octagonal dome, surrounded by a verandah supported on twenty eight columns. The opening has a muslim style foliated arch and the base, which has corresponding openings, is ascended by two separate staircases of fifteen steps each.

KHULDABAD

The taluka or district of Khuldabad consists of forty-four towns and villages. It is 22 kilometers from Aurangabad and it's area is 238 sq.km. It is also referred to as the 'Abode of Eternity' where many pious and holy saints are buried. It has immense historical and tourist value as Aurangzeb was buried at Khuldabad. In fact, Aurangzeb is remembered here as 'Khuldmakan'. After spending twenty-five years of his life in military campaigns in the Deccan, Aurangzeb according to his will, was buried in the courtyard of the tomb of Saint Zainuddin which was built by the Emperor himself during his lifetime.

Aurangzeb died as he had wished on 'Juma', Friday 21 February 1707 after saying his morning prayers. Well known for his piety, his grave conforms to his instructions saying that only Rs 4.5 he had recently earned, by the sale of caps he himself had sewn—a humble and holy pastime, should go towards the expenses of his funeral. He had also earned another Rs 305 by writing out copies of the Quran. It appears he was trying to make his peace with God in his later years. His grave does not exceed three yards in length, two and a half yards in breadth and a few inches in height. A small patch of earth in a cavity in the centre has a 'sabza' plant growing and there is no dome or roof

Emperor Aurangzeb Reading the Quran in His Old Age

over this grave. It is open to the sky. Its simplicity, after a century of such sumptuous Mughal tombs, reflects as intended, the difference between his character and that of his predecessors. It's air of poverty also symbolizes in a sense, the comparative value of the legacy he was handing to his successors. The Nizam of Hyderabad and Lord Curzon had the grave covered with marble, surrounded by a perforated marble screen. A plain white sheet is placed over the grave.

Khuldabad is also a famous pilgrimage centre. Two 'dargahs', situated on lofty platforms opposite each other house the 'Prophet's divine robes' and the 'Prophet's hair'. These are specially reserved for worship by devout pilgrims. Khuldabad also abounds with the tombs and mausoleums of nearly 1400 saints. It is believed that though the holy saints have physically died, their spirit lives on because they have reached 'Eternity'. In its popular form 'Sufism' is expressed mainly through the veneration of saints.

During 'Urs', annually held in Khuladabad, pilgrims arrive from all over the country and abroad to view the holy relics and sites. For its message of tolerance, Sufism has long been fashionable outside the Muslim world as well. In fact, throughout Islamic history, Sufis and mullahs have often clashed. Sufis stress tolerance through their poetry which mullahs generally shudder to read. Sufi's remember God by meditating on his name and reciting it even to the extent of sometimes going into a state of rapture.

The visiting pilgrims are housed in the many rooms surrounding the large open courtyards in the 'dargahs'. For the ablution rituals there are tanks of clear water available. At the main entrance is the 'Naqarkhana' or music hall where the 'Naubat' or music is played. This sleepy hamlet suddenly comes alive and is buzzing during 'Urs'.

The chief town of Khuldabad is Roza, which is surrounded by a high fortified wall built by Aurangzeb. It contains seven gates. The gateway on the Aurangabad side is approached by a steep, paved climb and it continues inside the city for about 300 feet. The sepulcher of Aurangzeb lies almost midway and one passes through a domed porch and gateway leading to an inner courtyard which in turn leads to Aurangzeb's grave. The town is remarkable as being the burial place of many distinguished persons other than Aurangzeb. Some of these are namely: Nizam-ul-mulk Asaf Jah, the founder of the Hyderabad dynasty, his son Nazir Jang, Nizam Shah the king of Ahmednagar and a host of others.

THE ROCK-CUT CAVE ARCHITECTURE

*The Greek satirist and sophist Lucien said
in the 2nd century A.D.
"Stone sculpted is Art and when scripted it is History"*

On a hunting expedition in 1819 in the wild mountainous terrain near Ajanta, a few soldiers of the British Army with Capt. John Smith were led by a cowherd to see some 'tiger lairs'. Thus, in the tradition of fairy tales, these forbidding, almost inaccessible grottos were discovered to be rich treasure caverns of the oldest Buddhist art in the world. Excavated on the south side of a horse shoe shaped ravine, approximately 106 km away from the main city of Aurangabad are the twenty-nine World Heritage Ajanta Caves. The Ajanta caves go as far back as 2nd century B.C., pre-Christian in date, upto the middle of 7th century A.D.

Indian art is primarily religious. It celebrates the Divine in the form of the Buddha, Shiva or Vishnu. However, the carvings of 'apsaras' or celestial nymphs on the walls and pillars delight the senses.

A.L. Basham vividly describes, 'Nearly all the artistic remains of ancient India are of a religious nature. Ancient India's religious art came chiefly from the hands of secular craftsmen. In the period between the Mauryas and the 'Golden Age of the Guptas', much wealth and energy was spent on Buddhist architecture. However, it was under the Satavahana Empire that the Vakatakas and their successors saw the chief architectural achievement in the form of the rock-cut caves of Ajanta. Few would dispute that the murals of Ajanta are among the greatest surviving paintings of any ancient civilization'.

Archaeological finds of very early Buddhist relics reveal that small wandering groups of Buddhist monks or 'Bhikshu's had gained a foothold in the Deccan. Based on the general assumption that a holy life is led in secluded and beautiful spots, Ajanta's lonely, hidden ravine was a suitable haven for Buddhist monastries. It also had the advantage of being near the flourishing trade centre of Pratishthana or modern day Paithan. The town of Paithan was barely 100 km away and on the route of rich merchants. These tradesmen prospered on lucrative trade with the West and travelled often from the hinterland to the seaport in Bombay.

Thus, the Sahyadri mountain range was chosen for the establishment of the cave temples. From whichever direction one may approach the Ajanta site, the enchantment is heightened by meeting the Waghora stream from its source to the series of waterfalls dropping some 30 metres, cutting out seven peculiar bowls of rock called the 'Sat Kund'.

AJANTA CAVES

The history of the Ajanta art of painting or rather of Indian art in its Buddhist form only commences about three and a half centuries after Buddha's lifetime. The missing links were perishable monuments built of bamboo and wood as these were the essential building materials of early settlers. There is historical reference to the 'wooden town' in the Indus Delta and also mentions of the splendours of the 'wooden palace' of the Maurya Emperor, Chandragupta Maurya. A super-structure of trimmed timber was set on a stylobate of stone, as can be seen today in the curvilinear roofs of these rock-cut caves. No wall painting, existed before stone came into use. Also, the earlier iconoclastic attitude of the Buddhist faith would not have allowed the creation of objects with sensuous appeal. In fact, the art was considered an indulgence of a luxurious life, very foreign to Buddhist monks. But this concept and form of self-denial could not survive and last forever among the monks and gradually, as Buddhism spread far and wide, Buddhist puritanism gave way to popular taste and folk art of the common people.

A secret charm of Buddhist Hindu sculpture is the profuse use of ornaments. The goddesses and apsaras wear jeweled earrings, necklaces, bangles and anklets, thus accentuating the charm of the female figure. Rene Grousset remarks. 'The nude female figures at Ajanta, with their flower-like grace, freedom of line and variety of attitude make them, as it were a poem of Hindu womanhood'.

Later, Emperor Ashoka's royal patronage of Buddhism encouraged further modification and with the passage of time, other forms were assimilated, carried down from antiquity. K.A. Nilakanta Sastri stated in 1952, 'Emperor Ashoka raised Buddhism to the status of an international religion, right from the position of a tribal and regional cult'. The Ajanta style of art echoes the artistic tradition of the Indus Valley in its representation of animals and birds, trees and flowers, the human torso and fabulous

Binoy K Behl

Overall view of Ajanta Caves

episodes of the Buddha's life as told by his followers. The monumental collection of some five hundred and forty-seven Jataka tales containing colourful legends of the many stories of the Buddha's life and his reincarnations are vividly painted here.

Eminent historian Karl Khandalavala had narrated, 'The story of Ajanta in the days of its finest achievements is that of vast walls teeming with painted life, where kings and princesses, and all the paraphernalia of great courts mingle with an unending stream of human activity. Tales of piety, charity and love are here, unfolded with the sweep and grandeur of a master's brush, in a spirit of reverence to the "Great One" who preached a faith that once brought light and hope to millions in India. They were humble men who

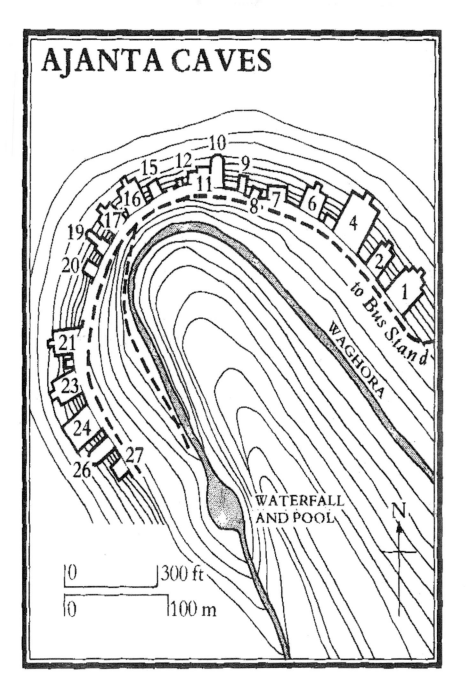

painted these scenes, but they had a vision which is given only to a few. Not a vision of God, but a vision of life itself in its varied manifestations.'

The cave paintings of Ajanta are often referred to as 'frescos', but this term is incorrect in the true sense of the word.

A fresco is painted while the plaster is still damp. The murals of Ajanta were made after the plaster had set. In the cave temples, the rough surface of the naked stone walls were first covered with a coating of potters clay, taken from the slimy beds of pools and mixed with molasses, cowdung, straw, rice husks or animal hair and perhaps, an animal glue as a binding medium. Roy Craven describes further, 'Once this was leveled to a thickness of about half an inch or more, it was coated with a smooth, fine, white, lime plaster which became the actual painting surface. On the still damp wall, the artist first laid out his composition with a red cinnabar line and then defined the subjects with an undercoat of grey or "terre verte". This was followed by the addition of local colours and once the whole wall was completely coloured, a brown or black line restated the drawing to finish the composition. A last burnishing with a smooth stone gave a rich lustrous surface. The colours which were natural and water-soluble, consisted of purple, brown, yellow, blue, white, green, red and black'. The artists worked in the dim caves by light reflected from outside by metal mirrors. John Griffiths said, 'There is a great deal in common between these paintings and the work of Egyptian and Italian artists of the 14th century. However, the intimate knowledge which the artists possessed of local life and living, with a general absence of foreign allusions, definitely defines that the artists were natives of India'. The first inhabitants of pre-historic India were 'Negroid' or 'Negrito' people. Some of these tribes still survive in the Andaman islands. According to R.C. Majumdar some of the 'Negrito elements or traits are depicted in Gupta art and sculpture and the Ajanta murals'. While clearly human in inspiration, Susan Huntingdon describes, 'Parts of the Bodhisattvas body are likened to other objects: the brow takes the shape of the archer's bow, eyes are like rose petals and the torso is shaped like that of a lion'. Often,

Binoy K Behl

Ajanta Cave No.1 - Bodhisattva Padmapani

scenes of Ajanta art take on an almost secular character, though all may be justified as being part of a Jataka tale or another Buddhist context. The narrow waists, full breasts and hips of the women in the composition, display the same feminine ideal that is found throughout most periods and styles of Indic art. On the other hand, 'From the common occurrence of Greek fretwork as an ornament, it has been thought likely that the artists may have belonged to the school of Bactrian Greeks.' Through overland trade exchanges, a cultural intercourse was facilitated, and the message of the Buddha left the shores of India enabling Buddhism to head towards becoming a world religion.

The Ajanta caves can clearly be divided into two groups, coinciding with the 'Hinayana' and 'Mahayana' phases of Buddhist art, spanning a period of about six centuries. After this period, excavations revived during the Vakataka reign especially their ruler Harishena (460–478). George Michell records, 'The series of paintings, mostly belonging to the later caves is unparalleled in the history of Indian art both for the wide range of subjects illustrated, and the assured mastery of the medium. Buddhist divinities and incidents from the life of the Master are shown many times. More vibrant are the episodes from the Jataka legends. These consist of large-scale crowded compositions depicting life in the court, town, hermitage or forest, with princes, consorts, attendants, musicians and servants. Never again did Indian mural painting exhibit such virtuosity and freedom'. The Ajanta caves are vital documents of Buddhist art. Walter Spink, a leading authority on Ajanta's later phase, argues convincingly that other writers are erroneous in their contention that such extraordinary achievements must have taken decades if not centuries to produce; instead he suggests that in a short burst of incredible artistic activity, during the Vakataka King Harishena's reign (460–478), the patrons, sculptors, painters, and iconographers provided the highest quality of Indic art. At Ajanta, religious devotion fused architecture, sculpture and painting into a unity and produced one of the great monuments of Buddhist art.

The Ajanta caves are not numbered chronologically but, for the sake of convenience, one can start from the cave at the outer most extremity.

CAVE 1: Late 5th century

This cave is the finest vihara of its kind, with the most ornamental façade decorated with sculpture. This Buddhist vihara is a rectangular hall with cells for monks on the inner sides leading out to a verandah which is 19.5 metres long and 2.8 metres wide. The ceiling which is 4.1 metres high is supported by twenty exquisitely carved and beautifully painted pillars. The brackets are richly ornamented with 'apsaras' and 'gandharvas'. By the latter part of the fifth to sixth century, the plan of the vihara included the function of the 'Chaitya' by introducing an imposing and colossal statue of a seated Buddha in a preaching pose or 'Vajra-Paryankasana' in place of the rounded stupa. Large areas of the walls and ceiling were once covered with paintings but are now damaged. However, some surviving important paintings are of the 'Bodhisattva Avalokitesvara' and the 'Miracle of Shravasti'. According to Yazdani, the 'Shakti Pandara', popularly known as 'the Black Princess' is one of the finest works of art in the world. No other portrait in Ajanta according to him, brings out this dark complexion set against a lighter background with such perfect eyes; the hazel-brown of the pupils and the red spot in the corners radiating an astonishing friendliness. The painting the 'Assault and Temptation of Mara' or the 'evil one' when temptation came to Gautama on the eve of his enlightenment, is another famous one. Other paintings on the ceiling are very decorative with floral, vegetal and animal motifs arranged in innumerable small panels.

CAVE 2: Late 5th century

This cave is another vihara similar to cave 1 but smaller, The verandah is 14.1 metres long and 2.4 metres wide. The façades at each end of the verandah are carved with 'Naga' Kings, their attendants and portly 'Ganas'. A richly carved doorway leads to an inner pillared hall. The roof is supported by twelve massive elaborately carved pillars. The twelve pillars have the minutest of carvings and profuse ornamentation. The back

Binoy K Behl

Ajanta Cave No.1 of 'King Mahajanaka' of Mithila

wall of the shrine is carved with a figure of Buddha in a teaching mode and on the left is Padmapani. This cave is remarkable for its painted ceiling. The painting takes the form of compartments filled in with a variety of large medallions, floral patterns, birds, fruit, flying figures, etc. Miniature seated Buddhas are painted on the side walls of the shrine, ante-chamber and hall. Nativity episodes, such as the dream of Maya, the birth of Gautama and other 'Jataka' tales cover the walls.

CAVE 3

This cave is a small, incomplete vihara of which only the preliminary excavation of the pillared verandah of approximately 9 metres in length was carried out. The work stopped after scooping out a rough entrance of the hall.

CAVE 4: Late 5th century

This is the largest monastery, planned on an ambitious scale at Ajanta but never completed. It has a verandah of approximately 27 metres by nearly 3.5 metres and 5 metres in height. The large entrance is one of the most elaborate at Ajanta. The lintel is decorated with little seated figures of Buddha and other sculptures. The hall has twenty-eight pillars arranged in a square. The shrine has a huge colossal Buddha in a teaching style flanked by Vajrapani and Padmapani. The walls of the antechamber are carved with six gigantic standing figures of Buddha. These figures of Buddha, along with those in the shrine originally bore paintings, traces of which still linger in patches.

CAVE 5

This 'vihara' was also left unfinished. It has a richly carved doorway with female figures standing on 'makaras'.

CAVE 6: Late 5th century

This is a double-storeyed monastery. The verandah of the lower storey has disappeared. Much of the doorway and decoration has crumbled. This cave has a total of 16 cells. The figure of Buddha in a teaching pose is detached from the back wall. The shrine was originally painted with many figures of Buddha but not much remains.

At the back of the shrine is a carved image of Buddha in a preaching attitude with a deer on the pedestal. The walls of the shrine are carved with many standing figures of Buddha. In fact, there is a profusion of carved figures of Buddha in different attitudes on the walls, hall, antechamber and shrine. There are mural fragments on the antechamber walls such as the temptation of 'Mara' and the miracle of 'Sravasti'

CAVE 7: Late 5th century

This monastery differs from others in not having a hall but two small porticos supported by two heavy octagonal pillars. The shrine has a seated image of Buddha. Also there are six standing figures of Buddha in 'vara-mudra' carved on the walls of the shrine. Below them are seated figures of Buddha. Evidently, this cave was once painted all over but nothing survives today.

CAVE 8: Late 5th century

This monastery was excavated at the lowest level but its major part does not exist anymore.

CAVE 9: 1st Century B.C.

This cave is oblong on plan, it is a small 'chaitya-griha' with a well balanced façade, is divided into a nave, an apse and aisles by a colonnade of twenty three pillars. At the

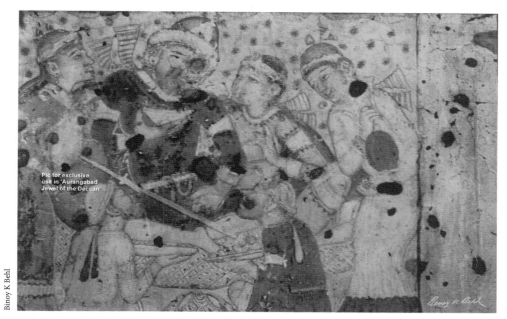

Ajanta Cave No.1 - A Bacchanalian Scene

Binoy K Behl

centre of the apse stands a globular stupa on a high cylindrical base. The crowning members are a railing and a 'Harmika'. Within the cave are two layers of paintings. It was a common practice amongst artists in ancient times to paint over an existing painting without completely rubbing it off. Remnants of old paintings still survive. A former painting shows the heads of two 'Bhikshus' with a recorded date of 5th century A.D. and another shows two 'Nagas' seated under a tree and one is multi-hooded. One painting shows a king listening to petitions from a group of five persons seated near his throne and another has a couple standing and a flying figure hovering towards the assembly.

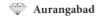

CAVE 10: 2nd century B.C.

This is among the first excavations at the site and is one of the most impressive early Buddhist 'Chaitya' hall. Like the preceding cave this one contains both the earlier and later phases of paintings. The subject matter of the paintings preserves the visit and worship of the 'Bodhi' tree and the stupa by a royal personage accompanied by his retinue of soldiers, dancers, musicians and women. Two of the 'Jataka' tales have been identified on the right wall.

CAVE 11: 5th century A.D.

The pillars here are somewhat clumsy and the cells irregular. The approach to the verandah and high plinth is by a flight of steps. The ceiling of the verandah is covered with painted motifs of flora, birds, beasts and geometric designs. The walls of the hall are painted mostly with figures of Buddha. The shrine has a Buddha image carved against an unfinished stupa. Large 'Bodhisattvas' are carved on either side of the doorway.

CAVE 12: 2nd century B.C.

This monastery is one of the earliest excavations and its front wall has totally disappeared. The paintings which once adorned the walls barely exist.

CAVE 13: 2nd century B.C.

This small monastery has completely lost it's front facade which has collapsed. There are no columns. There is no trace of any painting.

CAVE 14: 5th century A.D.

This cave was excavated at a higher level than the preceding one. It was planned on a large scale but has been left unfinished. The decoration of the verandah columns has now been reconstructed and differs from the others.

CAVE 15: 5th century A.D.

The pillars of the verandah of this monastery have fallen, leaving only the moulded plinth. The back wall of the shrine is carved with an image of Buddha seated on a 'Simhasana'. Above the doorway is a stupa sheltered by a canopy of serpent hoods. Traces of paintings on the ceilings can be seen.

CAVE 15A: 1st century B.C.

Descending by the flight of steps between caves 14 and 15, one finds to the right a small monastery consisting of a central hall flanked by a cell on each of its three sides. The walls of the hall above the cell doors are relieved with motifs like 'chaitya' windows rising from railings. There are elephants and a delicately modeled seated 'naga' deity.

CAVE 16: Late 5th century A.D.

This is one of the finest and most beautiful monasteries at Ajanta, combining elegance and architectural vigour. This vihara has a spacious verandah 19.5 metres long and 3.1 metres wide and is flanked by six octagonal pillars. An inscription on the left side wall outside the verandah furnishes the history of its excavation. It is recorded that this magnificent dwelling owes to the 'best of ascetics', Varahadeva, the minister of the Vakataka King Harishena (circa A.D. 475–500). Both sides of the main doorway have sculptures of beautiful women standing on 'makaras'. The dwelling was adorned by windows, doors, picture galleries, statues of celestial nymphs, ornamental pillars, stairs, a shrine and a 'Mandapa'. It was also provided with a large reservoir and a dwelling of the 'Lord of the Nagas'.

The hall has twenty pillars. There is no ante-chamber leading to the shrine. A gigantic image of a seated Buddha in a teaching attitude is carved in high relief and has a 'pradakshina-path' or circumambulatory passage around it.

Unfortunately, most of the paintings have disappeared. Of the few surviving compositions, one is noted for its masterly depiction of pathos in the painting of a beautiful princess dying. The famous painting of the 'Renunciation of Nanda' and the anxious maidens is beautifully revealed with emotion and eloquent hand gestures. Another painting depicts the 'Miracle of Sravasti' where Buddha multiplies himself into innumerable Buddhas in different mudras poised on lotuses in the presence of King Prasenjit of Sravasti. There is a painting of an elephant procession and another depicts Buddha preaching to a congregation. There are paintings devoted to illustrating incidents from the life of Buddha e.g. 'Sujata's offering of payasa', Buddha with his begging bowl, a sleeping figure of Maya, Gautama at school and practicing archery.

Two of the 'Jataka' tales can also be recognized—the first depicting where 'Bodhisattva' was born as a benevolent elephant, jumps down to his death from a great height in order to be served as food to hungry travelers. The feast of the elephant's carcass is shown. The second 'Jataka' story shows episodes of disputes being settled by Mahosadha—a famous tale is of two women fighting as to who was the real mother of a child and a judge ordering the child to be divided into two parts—a simple test in finding the real mother.

CAVE 17: Late 5th century A.D.

This vihara has a verandah which is 19.5 metres long and 3 metres wide with massive pillars in front. An inscription on the wall outside the verandah of this magnificent

Binoy K Behl

Ajanta Cave No.17 - Vishvantara Jataka

monastery owes its origin to the piety of the Vakataka King, Harishena. The doorway to the shrine is exquisitely carved with floral designs, Buddha figures, female doorkeepers, scroll-work, twisted rope design and lotus petals. The massive image of Buddha detached from the back wall of the shine is in a 'Dharmachakra mudra' or teaching attitude and is flanked by the figures of Padmapani and Vajrapani. Although the 61 distinct scenes which Burgess described many years ago no longer exist, this cave has preserved the greatest number of murals. The figures of the 'apsaras' and 'gandharvas' speak eloquently of the consummate skills of the artists. The flying figures of these 'apsaras' and gandharvas' produce a fantastic sense of movement, vitality and excitement. The walls of the hall are embellished with various 'Jataka' stories. It was a common practice with Ajanta artists to group episodes of a story according to the place of their occurrence and not necessarily in any sequence or a chronological order, e.g. stories of the Bodhisattva born as Prince Sutasoma, tales of the mischevious monkey, the elephant, the benevolent buffalo, the merciful stag and the *matsya* or fish. Many interesting incidents and miracles performed by Buddha are painted.

CAVE 18

This is merely a rectangular excavation, with two pillars and octagonal shafts, and most of it has collapsed.

CAVE 19: Late 5th century A.D.

This small, but architecturally well proportioned 'Chaitya-griha' made by the Vakataka King Harishena, is one of the most perfect specimens of Buddhist rock-cut architecture, It is a product of the fifth century A.D., but maintains the older style of the stupa with an elaborate, elongated drum and a globular dome. The only innovation is the introduction of the carved image of Buddha standing under and arch. It's crowning element is the 'Harmika'.

The walls of the hall are exquisitely painted with figures of Buddha where he is seen giving his begging bowl to Rahula who is standing by his mother Yashodhara. The ceilings are decorated with floral motifs interwoven with animals, birds and human figures. Very striking is a painting of an elephant fight.

CAVE 20: Late 5th century A.D.

This small monastery has been assigned to the period ranging from 450 A.D.–525 A.D. This cave has some innovations as the pillars of the verandah have bracket figures of graceful 'Sala-Bhanjikas, and the ceiling has imitation beams and rafters. The hall has no pillars. A narrow shrine has the carved image of Buddha in a teaching attitude. Unfortunately, most of the paintings have now disappeared.

CAVE 21: Late 5th century A.D.

The pillars of the verandah of this monastery have perished. The entablature above the pillars is carved with a 'Naga King' and his queen with attendants. The pillars of the hall survive, but they are somewhat heavy and disproportionate. The back wall of the shrine is carved in high relief with a seated figure of Buddha in a teaching attitude. Tragically, most of the paintings have perished. However, in the remaining fragments, the vividness of the blue lapis lazuli colour emerges.

CAVE 22: Late 5th century A.D.

This small monastery with a narrow verandah and four unfinished cells is approached by a flight of steps as it is on a higher level. Seven Manushi-Buddhas with Maitreya are painted under their respective Bodhi trees with their names written below each.

CAVE 23: Late 5th century A.D.

This cave has been left incomplete though the pillars of the verandah are intact. The pillars of the hall and porches display fine workmanship and ornamental details.

CAVE 24: Late 5th century A.D.

This monastery, if it had been completed, would have been very grand. The pillars of the verandah perished but have since been reconstructed and restored.

Binoy K Behl

Ajanta Cave No. 26 - Avalokitesvara

CAVE 25:

This small unfinished monastery has an enclosed courtyard, a pillared verandah and an astylar hall. There is no shrine.

CAVE 26: Late 5th century A.D.

This cave follows the general arrangement and decoration. The beauty of the façade is marred by the collapse of the pillared verandah. There are reliefs of Avalokitesvara with devotees praying.

There are two narrative scenes: one shows images of 'Mara' and a host of demons tempting Buddha with dance, music and other pleasures; another composition represents the 'Parinirvana' with a 7-metre figure of a reclining Buddha on a couch.

CAVE 27: Late 5th century A.D.

This cave cannot be called an independent cave as it really forms a part of Cave 26. On the right wall of the landing is the Rashtrakuta record outlining the use of these caves during the eighth and ninth centuries.

CAVE 28 and 29

Of the last two remaining caves, No. 28 is an unfinished monastery of which only the pillared verandah was excavated. No. 29 is a 'Chaitya-griha' in its first stage of excavation at the highest level. Both these caves are inaccessible.

BACK TO THE FUTURE

Taking a page out of the heritage books of other cities we find Barcelona, Spain, has completely transformed itself, thereby resulting in a huge tourist surge. Istanbul, Turkey, is another example where tourism flourished and spaces around its many monuments have all the facilities a tourist may need. The souks are bustling with visitors.

Unfortunately in India, sometimes tourists are seen clicking pictures sitting inside a taxi to avoid the unpleasant sights of open drains, piles of rubbish and an all pervading stench. However, this is going to change very soon as key issues in urban planning are being quickly sorted out in order to make our monuments more welcoming and tourist-friendly.

In Aurangabad, a 'Visitors Centre' has been built approximately 4 km before visitors arrive at the Ajanta Caves. This centre serves as an 'orientation' or 'interpretation' centre before the entry to the original monument. The centre was generously funded by the Japan Bank for International Co-operation or J.B.I.C., together with Ajanta Ellora Development project or A.E.D.P. A replica of four Ajanta Caves namely: Caves 1, 2, 16 & 17 is being built. The Times of India had quoted in its issue dated 27 December 2008 the following; 'The replica will ensure that visitors reaching the Ajanta Caves will not spend much time going through the original paintings all over again. 'Graham Brooks, an Australian expert in visitors management, who is part of the JBIC panel, had said during one of his visits to review the AEDP. The Maharashtra Tourism Development Corporation (MTDC) is the nodal agency for the AEDP.'

The Hindustan Times in its issue of 23 January 2009 reported. 'The Archaeological Survey of India has appointed Delhi based conservationist Gurmeet Rai for Ellora'. Rai advises that in the course of time, the Maharashtra Government should try to inscribe the entire surrounding area, including Daulatabad Fort as a 'World Heritage Complex'.

ELLORA CAVES

At a distance of only 29 km, in the opposite direction, very close to the city of Aurangabad are thirty-four World Heritage Ellora caves. These cave temples extend for more than a mile and they are carved in the crescent shaped scarp of the Jaina range of the Sahyadri mountains. The caves date from about 6th century and 10th century A.D. There are twelve Buddhist caves, seventeen Hindu caves and five Jain caves. In the last half of the sixth century, Ellora had become an important Hindu centre. The Buddhist caves were probably excavated during the 7th century, when the early Western Chalukyas had achieved supremacy in the Deccan. Control of the Deccan was taken from the early Western Chalukyas around 750 by the Rashtrakutas. Thus began a hegemony that was to last more than two hundred years until about 973. The political might of the Rashtrakuta empire is well acknowledged.

The Rashtrakutas were great patrons of art and architecture. The principal site associated with their artistic development is Ellora where several cave excavations were carried out under their aegis. Some historians believe that the Rashtrakutas gave their name to the country they ruled as the name 'Maharashtra' is derived from 'Rashtra-kutas'.

The first Englishman to see Ellora was Colonel John Seely of the Bombay Native Infantry in 1810. At that time, the caves were inhabited by beggars. He managed to chase them away and himself lived in one of the caves. John Seely thus describes the wonderland he had discovered, 'On a close approach to the temples, the eye and imagination are bewildered with the variety of interesting objects that present themselves on every side. The feelings are interested to a degree of awe, wonder and delight, that at first is painful, and it is a long time before they become sufficiently sobered and calm to contemplate with any attention, the surrounding wonders. The death like stillness of the place, the solitude of the adjoining plains, the romantic beauty

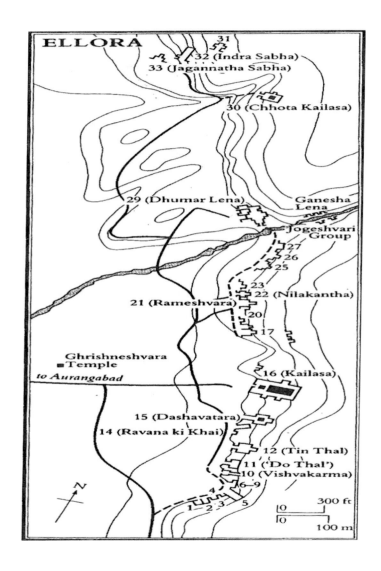

of the country, and the mountain itself perforated in every part, all tend to impress the mind of the stranger with feelings quite new, and far different from those felt in viewing magnificent edifices amidst the busy haunts of men. Everything here invites the mind to contemplation, and every surrounding object reminds it of a remote period and a mighty people, who were in a state of high civilization, whilst the natives of our own land were barbarians, living in woods and wilds'. About the Kailashanatha temple which impressed him the most he wrote: 'Conceive the burst of surprise at suddenly coming upon a stupendous temple, within a large open court, hewn of solid rock, with all its parts perfect and beautiful, standing proudly alone upon its native bed and detached from the neighbouring mountain by a spacious area all round. To build the Pantheon, the Parthenon at Athens, St Peters at Rome, our own St. Pauls or a Fonthill Abbey, is a task of science and labour; but we understand how it is done, how it proceeds and how it is finished; but to conceive for a moment a body of men however numerous, with a spirit, however invincible and resources however great, attack a solid mountain of rock, in most parts approximately 31 metres high and excavate by the slow process of the chisel, a temple like the one I have faintly described, with its galleries, or Pantheon—its vast area and indescribable mass of sculpture and carving in endless profusion—the work appears beyond belief and the mind is bewildered in amazement'.

When rock-cutting activity began in Western India, the artisans had no previous experience of excavating caves, and yet, India's temples often humble viewers with their grandeur and complexity. These artisans were basically trained as carpenters, who were now working in stone. The early rock cut caves are just copies of wooden structures in stone. This practice decreased with the passage of time and experience.

It is convenient to start with the twelve Buddhist caves first, as Cave 1 to Cave 5 were in the first phase of excavation 450–600 A.D. Cave 1 is close to the road from Aurangabad.

For the sake of convenience descriptions of all the Ellora caves will follow in numerical order.

CAVE 1: 7th century

It is probably the oldest 'Vihara' at Ellora, but is in ruins.

CAVE 2: 7th century

This is a large cave, The entrance to the cave is flanked by 'dvarapalas' wearing elaborate head-dress and a female figure of 'Tara', the Buddhist goddess, holds a lotus in her left hand, female attendants and flying 'vidyadharas' are in between. There are twelve massive pillars with square bases and cushion capitals.

A flight of steps leading to a verandah towards the north end has a pot bellied seated figure of 'Jambhala', the Buddhist god of wealth. The shrine in the back wall is flanked by huge Bodhisattvas and 'Padmapani' on the left and 'Vajrapani' on the right. The shrine contains a colossal Buddha image seated on a lion throne in a preaching attitude or 'dharmachakra-pravartana mudra' meaning turning the wheel of Law.

CAVE 3: 7th century

This is a 'vihara' where monks lived. The structure is incomplete, squarish on plan, and is supported by twelve pillars with square shafts. There are twelve cells. An unfinished carved Buddha with attendants is on the left wall. In a small chapel, on the left of the verandah, a Buddha is seated in a cross legged posture, or 'padmasana' on a lotus seat.

To the right are 'Bodhisattvas'. In the Buddhist pantheon, 'Bodhisattvas' are divinities who have not yet reached the state of the Buddha. Merchants and traders who had to transport goods over long distances, worshiped 'Bodhisattvas' to save them from the eight great dangers they may encounter on the way namely: fire, dacoits, chains, shipwreck, lions, cobras, elephants and even death. All this is depicted in the panel with 'Avalokiteshvara' protecting his devotees.

CAVE 4: 7th century

This double storied cave is largely in ruins. On the left is an image of a seated 'Padmapani' holding a rosary in his right hand, a lotus in his left and wears deer skin on his left shoulder. Female attendants are around. In the back wall is a shrine which has a seated Buddha in a teaching attitude, tall attendants and female fly whisk bearers wearing heavy, elaborate jewellery.

CAVE 4: (Upper)

This cave is in a dilapidated condition in ruins.

CAVE 5: 7th century

This cave is locally known as 'Maharwada' indicating that for sometime it was occupied by people belonging to the Mahar caste, a backward community in Maharashtra. It is a large vihara with cells in the side walls. The large hall is supported by twenty-four massive pillars with square shafts and cushion capitals. In the small shrine, is a seated Buddha, with female attendants wearing elaborate jewellery.

CAVE 6: 7th century

Cave No. 6 is in a dilapidated condition. The most interesting is the south side depicting a goddess with a peacock identified with the Buddhist goddess 'Mahamayuri'.

CAVE 7: 7th century

This cave is a ruined vihara.

CAVE 8: 7th century

This cave can be entered from Cave 7 through a roughly cut passage. The hall has a 'Padmapani' with attendants and a number of 'Vidyadharas'. The shrine has a circumambulatory passage. At the south end there is an image of 'Mahamayuri' similar to Cave 6.

On the north is a chapel with Buddha flanked by attendants and Vajrapani with a female attendant. This cave can be assigned the date of 700 A.D. because it resembles a later cave i.e. cave 14 'Ravana-ki-khai' in its plan.

CAVE 9: 7th century

This cave is in a ruined state and what remains is a highly embellished façade and a panel with Buddhist goddess Tara. She is a very important deity in the Buddhist pantheon. In the panel is a snake, a sword, an elephant, a fire and a shipwreck. This is the only litany of Tara in western India

CAVE 10: (Vishvakarma) 7th century

Locally known as 'Vishvakarma' or 'Sutar-ka-jhopda' (meaning carpenter's hut), this cave is the finest of the Buddhist group at Ellora. It is the only 'chaitya-griha' or a prayer hall in the Buddhist group and is also adorned with exquisite sculptures. The pillared verandah of the chaitya has a small shrine at either end and a single cell in the far end of the back wall.

Professor M.K. Dhavalikar lucidly describes: 'The corridor pillars have massive squarish shafts and vase-and-foliage (ghatta-pallava) capitals. This type of capital is characteristic of the Gupta period, which is referred to as the 'Golden Age' in Indian history. The vase (ghata) filled with foliage (pallava) is a symbol of prosperity in Hindu mythology.

Ellora Cave 10

The façade of the cave is very impressive. The temple has an upper storey over the entrance which was perhaps, the musicians gallery. It has a pillared verandah, crowned by a fully developed trefoil arch flanked by Vidyadharas and attendants. On the parapet of the gallery are carved human couples in the upper band and elephants in the lower.

The learned Professor continues, 'The main hall is very spacious and high. It is apsidal on plan and is divided into a central nave and side aisles by twenty eight octagonal pillars with plain bracket capitals. The triforium over the pillars of the nave is divided into compartments that contain Buddha figures in the dharma-chakra-

Ellora Cave 10

pravartana mudra (turning the wheel of law) and in a preaching attitude as well. Buddha is flanked by attendants and dwarfs below. In the apsidal end of the hall is a stupa, on the face of which is carved in a recessed arch, a massive squarish colossal Buddha about 3.30 mts high, seated in a European fashion with his feet hanging down. At the back is a huge 'Bodhi' tree or 'ficus religiosa' below which the Buddha gained enlightenment. The hall has a vaulted roof which gives an echo effect. There are naga busts carved on the walls. On the right is a carved image of Avalokiteshvara, attendants, Vidyadharas and Manjusri in the north, 'Tara' is holding a lotus and there are other Buddha figures and another one of Avalokiteshvara with attendants.

CAVE 11: (Do Thal) 8th century

This cave is locally known as 'Do Thal' which means double storied but actually consists of three stories as a lower-level ground floor was discovered. It has a spacious rock-cut fort in front. To the left is a shrine of 'Avalokiteshvara' seated on a lion throne, a female figure and Tara seated cross-legged on either side, and a four armed 'Devi' on his left. On the right wall is a Buddha whose head is smashed but flanked by two Bodhisattvas and two chauri-bearers. Images of Hindu deities Durga and Ganesha, also appear, which implies that these were later additions. The ground floor has a long pillared verandah with a shrine in the middle of the back wall containing a Buddha figure flanked by Padmapani and Vajrapani. A staircase on the left leads to the upper floor.

The first floor has a long pillared verandah with two unfinished shrines and a finished third one where the back wall contains a huge seated image of Buddha. A female devotee, 'Sujata', is offering Buddha food whilst another is seen prostrating before him. Buddha himself is in the 'Bhumi-sparsha-mudra' flanked by Padmapani and Vajrapani with his thunder-bolt. The side walls are covered with figures of Bodhisattvas e.g. 'Maitreya' with a miniature stupa in his crown, 'Sthirachakra' holding a sword and Jnanaketu with a pennan. Above them are the figures of 'Jambhala', the Buddhist God of wealth and Tara holding a lotus near a man with a pot of coins.

A flight of steps leads to the top floor which again consists of a pillared verandah and a shrine in the centre of the back wall. There is an image of Buddha with his attendants. On the walls are figures of many small Buddhas.

CAVE 12: (Tin Thal) 8th century

Professor M.K. Dhavalikar has vividly described this cave as one of the most important Buddhist edifices in India and can be assigned to 700 A.D. 'Like cave 11, it is another three-storied cave known as 'Tin Thal'. The ground floor consists of a large hall, an oblong

Ellora Cave 12

vestibule and a shrine. The hall has eight pillars in three rows. The back wall has a sculpture in nine panels representing the 'Mandala' or magic diagram of the 'cosmos' as Buddhists see it. In the centre is a seated Buddha with fly whisk bearers and Padmapani and Vajrapani. The upper row has a seated 'Bodhisattva or Rakta Lokeshvar', a 'Sthirachakra' holding a sword and a third is 'Jnanaketu' holding a flower stalk. The bottom row again has a Jnanaketu holding a Lotus stalk and the third is 'Manjusri'. The images of all the Bodhisattvas cannot be identified with certainty but they all wear rich jewellery'.

On the north side are rock-cut beds for monks. On the right and left of the vestibule are Buddha images on lion seats and attendants holding lotus flowers.

Ellora Cave 12

Smaller panels depict 'Vajrasattva', 'Padmapani', 'Vajrapani' and 'Tara'. The left wall panel shows Buddha and the four armed Buddhist goddess, 'Chunda'. Her usual attributes are 'abhaya mudra' or granting protection, holding a rosary, a bowl, a ladle, and wearing a cylindrical head-dress.

The shrine door has a 'Maitreya' on the right and 'Manjusri' on the left. The shrine itself has a colossal image of Buddha and on the side walls are five 'dhyani' or meditating Buddhas. Below them are large figures of Padmapani holding a lotus, 'Jnanaketu' with a flag, and 'Sthirachakra' with a sword and 'Triratna', a fourth holding a lotus and a fifth is mutilated.

Ellora Cave 12

Prof. Dhavalikar further elaborates on the twelve cells that exist in the hall of this cave. From the first cell, a staircase leads to the first floor to a chamber with two pillars and several carved sculptures. On the back wall is a Buddha seated on a throne flanked by attendants, male and female. The stairs continue towards a long verandah leading to a hall. The hall is divided into three aisles by two rows of massive pillars and many sculptures including a Buddha, Padmapani with female devotees and a stupa.

The shrine is flanked by guardians. The north has Padmapani holding a full blown lotus and the south has Vajrapani with his thunderbolt. The jewellery they wear is elaborate and the jeweled belts are elegant. Inside the shrine is a seated Buddha in front

Ellora Cave 12

of whom is a female devotee, 'Sujata', offering food to him. On the side walls are four figures and above are seen seven seated Buddhas.

As we move from the far northern end of the verandah, stairs lead to the top floor. There are more figures, including a seated Buddha, and on his seat is a carved wheel or 'dharmachakra' with deer on either side. A standing Buddha can also be seen.

The top floor of the cave is complete and is very impressive. This gives clear evidence that when these caves were excavated, work always started from the top and went downwards to the ground floor, which was the last to be carved and often remained unfinished. The top floor consists of a spacious hall, with a vestibule and a shrine in the back wall. The hall is divided into five aisles by five rows of massive squarish pillars. On the side walls are recesses at the end, containing large sculpted panels depicting Buddha seated on a throne in a preaching or 'vyakhyana mudra'. Another panel shows Buddha in a meditating posture or 'dhyan mudra'; Buddha preaching his Law to go to heaven and Buddha entering 'Nirvana'. There are more sculptures on the right, and on the left side is a row of seven 'manushi' Buddhas in a meditating pose, each with his particular sacred tree and a halo at the back. The same occurs in Cave 22 at Ajanta.

According to Buddhist texts these particular sacred trees are the following:
1) Patali or trumpet flower
2) Pundarika, sweet smelling mango
3) Shala (Shorea robusta)
4) Shirisha (Acacia sirisa)
5) Udumbara (Ficus glomorata)
6) Nyagrodha (Ficus indica)
7) Pippala (Ficus religiosa)

On the right side of the back wall are seven seated Buddhas shown in a teaching attitude with a nimbus at the back and an umbrella over their heads.

They are Bodhisattvas namely:
1) Vairochana
2) Akshobhya
3) Ratnasambhava
4) Amitabha
5) Amoghasiddhi
6) Vajrasattva
7) Vajraraja

On the side and back walls of the vestibule are twelve goddesses seated on lotuses:

1) Vajradhatvishvari holding a chintamani or jewel
2) Chunda holding a lotus with a book.
3) Three representations of Tara:
    a. Khadiravani seated on a lotus holding a lotus stalk held by two cobra figures.
    b. Another holding a lotus stalk held by a cobra beside which there is a swan.
    c. The third figure is indentical.
4) Janguli is an interesting female figure as her wrist band and head-dress are made of cobras.
5) Mahamayuri with a peacock feather in her left hand.
6) Ushanishavijaya holding a water vessel or 'kamandhalu'
7) Bhrikuti
8) Pandara
9) Tara

The most striking feature of this cave is that it is profusely decorated with sculptures of Buddhist goddesses. Buddha himself was totally opposed to women being admitted in the monastic order and for a very long time, there were no nuns in Buddhist establishments. The 'Hinayana' sect of Buddhism strictly followed the teaching of the 'Enlightened One'. With the rise of the 'Mahayana' sect at the beginning of the Christian era, first the Buddha and then Bodhisattva images came to be worshipped. Later, women were admitted to the 'Order' and as a consequence, goddesses were created namely 'Tara'. Buddhism was now beginning to compete with Hinduism and its images of it's pantheon of gods and goddesses. Also, new goddesses appeared in the Buddhist pantheon, and the occurrence of so many of them, led to the emergence of Tantric Buddhism in Western India. Finally, it was the dominance of Tantricism which led to the decline of Buddhism in India.

Cave 13

This is totally destroyed.

HINDU CAVES

Situated in the middle of the complex between the Buddhist and Jain groups are sixteen Brahmanical or Hindu caves. The Hindu pantheon evolved in the fifth and sixth centuries A.D., when Hinduism received the royal patronage of the Imperial Guptas.

This was the period of the Puranas, the epics of Mahabharata and Ramayana and the rise of the Bhakti cult. The three most important cults are Shaivism, Vaishnavism and Shaktism in Hinduism. The caves at Ellora have numerous panels illustrating a number of divinities, Puranic legends and scenes from the epics.

CAVE 14: (Ravana-ki-khai) early 7th century

This cave is locally known as 'Ravana-ki-Khai' or Ravana's pit. It is a squarish hall supported by sixteen pillars. At the back is an oblong shrine with a circumambulatory passage around it. Prof. Dhavalikar has given a very detailed description of this cave namely: The pillars have elaborate decoration. The walls of the cave are almost fully covered with exquisite sculptures.

Starting from the front north wall:

1) Goddess Durga, her foot over a lion, her mount; she is four-armed with a trident or trishul in her upper right hand.

2) Lakshmi, the consort of Vishnu, seated over lotuses in which cobra-kings are holding water jars. A tortoise is also seen. She has two arms, but her attendants have four, one of them is holding a conch, an attribute of Vishnu. Elephants are seen bathing the Goddess with water jars and therefore, she is identified as Gaja-Lakshmi.

3) The Boar or Varaha is an incarnation of Vishnu, with his foot on the serpent Shesha. He holds Prithvi, the earth goddess whom he saves from destruction.

4) Vishnu is shown in this panel in his abode, 'Vaikuntha' with his consorts 'Sridevi' and 'Bhudevi'. Four attendants are holding fly whisks and below is an eagle, the God's mount, a few male and female figures playing musical instruments. Below are six human figures, two male and four female.

5) In this panel, Vishnu and Lakshmi are seated under an arch with attendants. Below them are seven dwarfs holding musical instruments.

The proper shrine at the back has 'dvarpalas', a number of devotees, a male dwarf or 'gana', a female dwarf or 'vamanika', and Ganga on a crocodile to the right and Yamuna on a tortoise to the left. They all wear elaborate jewellery, the folds of their garments are depicted very realistically.

The altar has a broken image of Durga and perhaps this shrine was dedicated to her. On the floor are holes that may have been fire pits.

In the south-east corner of the circumambulatory passage is a carved 'Virabhadra' with a battle axe and a small drum or damru. On his seat is carved a bull, his mount. Vira Bhadra is an extremely fierce form of Shiva. The 'mount' or 'vahana' for Shiva is the 'bull' or 'nandi'. Sacred animals served as a means of transportation for Shiva. There are seven mother goddesses on the north side, and 'Ganesha' and 'Kali'. They all wear lavish jewellery and a tall head-dress. The goddesses can be identified from their mounts carved on their pedestals:

1) Chamunda (owl)
2) Indrani (elephant)
3) Varahi (boar)
4) Vaishnavi (eagle)
5) Kaumari (peacock)
6) Maheshwari (bull)
7) Brahmi (swan)

The south wall panel depicts the 'Andhakasura vada murti' form of Shiva. He is shown with eight hands and the right one holds 'andhakasura' and the four are stretching the elephant skin over his head. The story narrates that when Shiva wanted to annihilate the demon Andhaka, the latter's friend Gajasura in the form of an elephant attacked Shiva, who slayed him first. Parvati, Shiva's consort, his son Ganesha and a dwarf are also present.

The next panel depicts Ravana, the ten headed demon king, shaking Shiva's abode, Mount Kailash. Shiva is about to crush Ravana with his toe but the latter begs his forgiveness. Shiva relents and lets him go.

In the next panel, Shiva is seen dancing the 'Tandava'. Hindu mythology acknowledges Shiva as the master of dance, hence 'Nataraja'. Three drummers can be seen to the left, Parvati and two dwarfs to the right. Bhringi, who is Shiva's devotee, Indra on an elephant, Agni on a ram and Brahma and Vishnu also.

The dancing Shiva is well known in Indian art and the story narrates that Shiva went to the forest to defeat the holy sages in a debate. The sages got angry and created a tiger who pounced upon Shiva, who killed it and wore the tiger skin. The sages next sent a snake which Shiva wore as an ornament. Lastly, the sages sent a demon and Shiva trampled upon him and started dancing. This is the 'apasmara purusha' seen under Shiva's feet in these dancing panels.

The next panel shows Shiva and Parvati playing a game of chausar or dice. Ganesha, the elephant-headed son of Shiva, two attendants male and female, a number of dwarfs, Nandi the bull, and the mount of Shiva can all be identified. Shiva is four armed and one hand is shown holding the hand of Parvati.

CAVE 15: (DASHAVATARA) Mid 8th century

Several steps lead to this cave as it is at a much higher level. The cave is called 'Dashavatara' or ten incarnations of Vishnu. There is a spacious rock-cut court in front, in the centre

Ellora Cave 15

of which is a free standing monolithic 'mandapa', and small shrines and a cistern. The pavilion has a small porch in front, supported by two square pillars. The west wall has a perforated window over which a Sanskrit inscription is engraved in the Brahmi script giving the genealogy of the Rashtrakuta dynasty. This cave is a double storeyed cave, it is quite spacious, supported by fourteen square pillars and the upper floor is supported by forty-four pillars exquisitely carved. There are sculptures of Ganesh, Surya, Vishnu, Ardhanarishvara, Durga slaying the buffalo demon Mahishasura and the marriage of Shiva and Parvati with Brahma seated as the three headed priest. The ten incarnations of Lord Vishnu are aesthetically carved. The sculptures are of gigantic proportions, bursting out of their frames releasing tremendous charged up emotion, force and energy. These qualities are very characteristic of Rashtrakuta art.

Ellora Cave 15

CAVE 16: (Kailasa) or the Abode of Shiva Mid 8th century and later

Architecturally and sculpturally, this is perhaps the finest cave temple in the world, representing the climax of rock-cut Indian architecture. Though locally it is referred to as Kailas, it is in effect the world's largest monolithic structure.

According to legend, the Queen of the Rashtrakuta King Elu wanted to build a magnificent temple of Shiva and she vowed to fast and not partake of any food until she saw the finial of the temple.

The king invited architects from different parts of the country, and an architect from nearby Paithan by the name of Kokasa undertook the task of carving the finial in

Ellora Cave 16

no time. This was possible because in cave excavations, the work always starts from the top and proceeds downwards.

The queen had to give up her fast. It is a well known fact that sometimes when people are unable to enter a temple, they prostrate before the finial or Kalasha over the spire or shikara from a distance.

The Rashtrakutas being great patrons of art and architecture, were also great builders. Rashtrakuta King Krishna l (757–72) built the world famous Kailash temple at Ellora. This massive structure is carved out of a single solid granite rock about 100 feet high and is a remarkable engineering feat of the 8th century. The temple measures 46 metres x 31 metres. Vincent Smith extols it as the most marvelous architectural wonder of the world.

Ellora Cave 16

Dr Percy Brown observes 'The temple of Kailasa at Ellora is not only the most stupendous single work of art executed in India, but as an example of rock architecture, it is unrivalled. The Kailasa is an illustration of one of those occasions when men's minds, hearts and heads work in unison towards the consummation of a supreme ideal', Kailasa has been described as an 'epic in stone'. If poetry can be written in stone, this is it!

The poet who wrote the inscription at Ellora fancies that even the denizens of heaven were awe stricken by its grandeur, whispering among themselves, 'This must be the creator's miracle and not a human performance, otherwise how could it be so perfect and magnificent!'

Kailasa is a combination of the southern and northern styles. It has a strong Dravidian complex with a 'gopuram', a 'Nandi mandapa' the 'vimana' and surrounding cloisters.

Ellora Cave 16

The temple complex Gopura, is situated on the ground level with a high rock-cut screen at the front with carved sculptures of 'dikpalas' or guardians of directions and river goddesses. Many of these are badly mutilated.

From the north, in the first panel only, the outline has been incised. The second has Shiva with ten hands and the third Brahma. On the western wall is the Lingodbhava-murti emphasizing Shiva's superiority over Vishnu and Brahma with the lingam in the centre. Next is a four armed Shiva holding a trident or trishul. 'Kartikeya' is seen on a peacock, Arjuna in the guise of a mendicant abducting Subhadra and the ensuing battle between Arjuna and Balarama, Subhadra's brother. There is 'Agni' on ram, 'Vayu' on a stag and 'Varuna' on crocodile. On the back wall is a finely carved 'naga' or cobra couple and a female dwarf. There are the river goddesses, Ganga on a crocodile and

Yamuna on a tortoise. On the right is Yama or God of death on a buffalo, Vishnu on a garuda and again Vishnu as Vamana or Trivikrama because he covered the three worlds in three gigantic strides.

Two other panels show Shiva dancing the Tandava and the man-lion Narsimha incarnation of Vishnu. However, these are all damaged.

At the entrance of the spacious court which surrounds the temple, there is a free standing Nandi pavilion on a highly decorative base. A panel facing the entrance depicts Gaja Lakshmi seated in a lotus pond, symbolizing prosperity being bathed by elephants. Monolithic columns approximately 17 metres high with elaborate mouldings stand on either side. Two elephants, three dimensional with broken trunks are nearby.

There is the eight armed Durga slaying the buffalo demon and there are the gods above in the sky namely, Indra, Vayu, Yama, Agni, Kubera, Varuna and flying Vidyadharas. Another panel depicts Krishna lifting mount Govardhan with one finger. Next is Vishnu followed by Lakshmi.

In the spacious courts on the north and south of the main temple one is awed by carvings of huge elephants and victory pillars. There is a very large artistic and dramatic sculpture depicting multi-armed Ravana shaking Kailas the abode of Shiva and Parvati, exerting all his might and power. But Shiva, by just pressing his foot on the mountain, frustrates Ravana's evil designs. Coomaraswamy observes: 'In no other art have geotectonic conceptions been realized with such power as here'. As the mountain shakes, Parvati clutches Shiva's arm in fright. Her emotional tension is expressed through pose and gesture in a remarkable way. Many scenes from Lord Krishna's life and scenes from the two epics Ramayana and Mahabharata intricately carved can be seen.

There are life size sculptures of amorous couples in erotic postures as well.

CAVE 17: Late 6th century

At a considerable distance away is cave 17 hugely damaged by landslides.

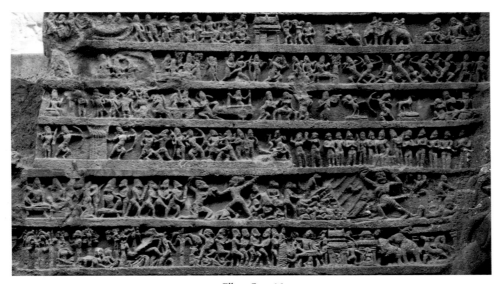

Ellora Cave 16

CAVE 18 : Late 6th century

This cave too is in a similar condition but has a shrine with a Shiva Linga.

CAVE 19

This cave is incomplete and damaged.

CAVE 20 A

This cave is very plain and largely destroyed.

CAVE 20 B

This cave is largely destroyed,

CAVE 21: (Rameshvara) Middle to late 6th century

This was one of the early caves to be excavated at Ellora and is one of the finest rock-cut temples in India. In the courtyard is a pedestal with a monolithic Nandi decorated with figures of gods and goddesses.

This cave is renowned for the sensuous beauty of its fully modelled sculptures. Colossal, more than life-size images of females and amorous couples stand out as the finest of their class. The alluring curves of the figures are in the Vakataka-Gupta tradition.

CAVE 22: (Nilakantha) 8th century

The cave is known as 'Blue throated' or 'Nilakantha', which is one of the names of Shiva. The cave consists of a shrine, a vestibule, a pillared hall and a destroyed Nandi pavilion.

CAVE 23 and 24

These are only very small shrines.

CAVE 25: (Kumbharwada) Potters Quarter or Sureshwar

This cave consists of a squarish shrine, a vestibule, a pillared hall and vestibules on the sides. A large portion of the hall is destroyed. On the ceiling is an image of Surya, hence the name of the cave Sureshwar.

Ellora Cave 21

CAVE 26: (Janawasa) late 6th century

This cave consists of a hall with pillars and a wall panel of Brahma, Vishnu and Mahesh.

CAVE 27

This cave is completely ruined.

CAVE 28

This cave is located on the edge of a ravine but is in a completely ruined condition.

Ellora Cave 26

CAVE 29: (Dhumar Lena) late 6th century

This cave is known as 'Dhumar Lena' and also 'Sita ki Nahani' as it is located near a waterfall. It is one of the largest caves in Western India and in plan resembles the main cave at Elephanta near Mumbai. A low flight of steps leads to the hall which is supported by four rows of massive pillars with massive square shafts and cushion capitals.

The entire cave is adorned with large sculptured panels containing mammoth sized figures. An outstanding composition of the marriage of Shiva and Parvati in the presence of the gods is on the eastern wall. Towards the back wall is an independent shrine in a detached square sanctuary containing a Shiva linga which can be circumambulated. Also, a wall shows Shiva dancing the 'Tandava'.

Ellora Cave 29

GANESHA LENA

Just above cave 29 at a distance of about 100 metres is located a group of small shrines known as 'Ganesha Lena'. Traces of some paintings survive on the ceilings. It could be assigned a date after about the 9th century.

JAIN GROUP

The Jain Group at Ellora consists of only five caves and belongs to the ninth and tenth centuries. These caves were probably excavated during the reign of the Rashtrakuta King Amoghavasha (819–81). The founder of Jainism was Mahavira, a senior

Ellora Cave 29

contemporary of Buddha and one of the twenty-four Tirthankaras. The Jain caves belong to the 'Digambara', or 'sky-clad sect'. The figures are quite repetitive and are shown not wearing any clothes.

CAVE 30: (Chhota Kailasa) early 9th century

It is called Chhota Kailasa as it is a replica of Cave 16 on a small scale and is incomplete. There is a columned mandapa, entered through a porch, and a shrine at the back. Twenty-two seated 'Tirthankaras' are located in the mandapa. An image of Mahavira seated on a lion throne is enshrined within the sanctuary. There are traces of paintings on the ceiling.

CAVE 31

This small cave is unfinished. It consists of a four pillared hall and a shrine. Inside the shrine is Lord Mahavira, the founder of Jainism.

CAVE 32: (Indra Sabha), early 9th century

This cave is the most interesting and ornate of the Jain caves; it is a double storeyed cave. The walls are heavily sculpted with images of 'Parshvanath' whose distinguishing attribute is a seven hooded cobra and an umbrella over his head, held by a female attendant. Parshvanath was Mahavira's senior.

The ground floor consists of a hall with a double verandah. It is supported by twelve squarish pillars. A flight of stairs leads to the upper floor hall supported by twelve elegantly carved pillars. The walls have images of 'Tirthankaras' and Jinas'. Exuberant foliate and garland motifs are carved on the fluted shafts and capitals of the columns. A beautiful lotus is carved on the ceiling of the shrine. A magnificent 'yakshi' is seated on her lion under a mango tree laden with fruit. Fragments of paintings survive on the ceiling.

CAVE 33: (Jaganatha Sabha) 9th century

This is the last cave at Ellora and it's name literally implies 'the court of the Lord of the World'. It consists of five independent shrines, each with a columned mandapa and sanctuary, and it is on two levels. There are paintings on the ceiling and also on the walls. The paintings comprise of geometric patterns and 'Jinas' with their devotees.

CAVE 34: 9th century

This small cave is approached through an opening on the left side of cave 33. There are no sculptures in the verandah but there is a shrine of 'Mahavira'. On the side walls are 'Parshvanath' and Gomateshvara'.

Parshvanath Cave

At some distance from the last Jain cave, is located yet another cave, that contains a colossal image of 'Parshvanath', hence its name. The image of 'Parshvanath' is shown seated on 'Simhasana' or a lion seat. 'Simhasana' is about 3 metres in height and has seven cobra hoods over its head, flanked by devotees.

AURANGABAD CAVES

Two miles west of the city of Aurangabad, and seven hundred feet high, the Aurangabad caves are situated in the Sahyadri range of the Western Ghats of Maharashtra. While these shrines are lesser known, they are aesthetically very significant and they afford penetrating insights concerning the development of Buddhism in India during the 5th and 6th century A.D.

Over a hundred years have passed since Burgess made a report in regard to these caves, especially Cave 9. 'The apartments at the east end of the hall are choked up with mud and seem to be frequented by wild beasts. Much water stands in the whole of these rooms during the rains and they are unpleasant to remain in for any time'. In 1914, Yazdani found the caves very difficult to access and much repair was needed. Today, the situation is quite different. With assiduous implementation of preservation and administrative efforts, tourists from all over the world visit these caves frequently.

There are nine caves in all, 'carved into the mountain side Deccan trap scarp which is a basaltic lava covering an original granite and gneiss base'. Since time immemorial, the hills of Aurangabad had been occupied for devotional purposes. The Aurangabad caves were built as monastries or viharas in the 5th and 6th centuries and served as both, a dwelling and places of worship. They are assigned to the Vakataka and Kalachuri periods. Nearby is a tributary of the Godavari river, and during the monsoon, water rushes down the hills in gushing streams. At the foot of these hills, the Archaeological Survey has found stone cut reservoirs measuring five feet by 10 feet for drinking water. There are no inscriptions whatsoever at the Aurangabad caves. However, Carmel Berkson observes, 'Tantric influences are in evidence in the concentration on the female, in the iconography which includes the diamond sceptre or thunderbolt or "vajra" in the three phases of Buddhist transformation "trikaya" and in the architectural

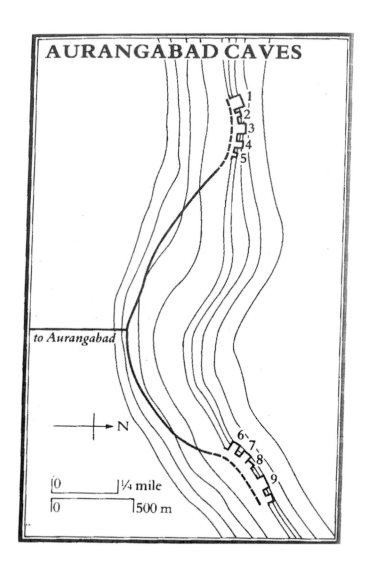

AURANGABAD CAVES

to Aurangabad

N

0 — ¼ mile

0 — 500 m

Exterior view of Cave No. 5, 6, 7 of Aurangabad Caves

design of the caves, some of which were constructed following the plan of the mandala, for circumambulation of the Buddha in the shrine'.

Susan Huntingdon observes, 'The female figures demonstrate a stylistic departure from the earlier Vakataka style adding new tautness to the contours of their bodies, which are full breasted, round hipped and have swelling thighs. Their elaborate coiffures are characteristic of the sixth century. The presence of prominent female imagery, especially the females as attendants to Bodhisattvas, demonstrates the growing importance of Tantric sects. From the spectacular imagery of a group of six female musicians and a dancing woman on a wall of the main shrine in Cave 7 we can

Cave No. 7 Buddha statue Garbha Gruh

conclude that esoteric and Tantric forms of Buddhism were in practice in Aurangabad in the sixth century'.

Tantric Buddhism in Tibet, Mongolia, Japan and China is based on the practice as it existed in India.

In Buddhism, the practice or rite of circumambulation was designed for the disciple or pilgrim to experience walking around the shrine uttering 'mantras' which aid in identifying the mystic individual 'Self' with the concept of Buddhahood. The devotee is in a constant quest to transform himself in order to ascend the spiritual sphere.

In fact, the architecture of the caves have superb acoustical effects which powerfully manifest when narrow pathways are circumambulated around the figure of the Buddha in the shrine. A low chanting of the sacred syllable 'Om' resonates in a deep and wonderful way.

Buddha Stupa

There are two main groups of Buddhist caves (Caves 1 to 5 and Caves 6 to 9 separated by about a distance of 1.3 km) belonging to the late 5th or early 6th century. There is another third group but these caves are unfinished and have no sculpture.

First Group or Southern Caves
Caves 1 to 5 at a height of 300 feet

CAVE 1: Late 5th century

This cave is situated near the top of the hill with eight elaborately carved columns. The columns are divided into sections. There are squarish blocks with dwarf-like playful creatures or 'ganas' at the corners, rounded with a vertical and horizontal ornamental band, riders on mythical animals or 'sardulas' and flying figures or 'vidyadharas', and

Dancing Tara with Attendants

carved bas-reliefs at the bases of the brackets. In addition there are loving couples or 'maithuna' in lotus medallions. The façade wall is pierced with windows, two small side doors and an elaborate central portal. Carved into the north and south wall of the outer porch, in large panels, Buddha sits on a broad lotus; the stalk is upheld by nagas. To the left is a relief of seven seated Buddhas flanked by Bodhisattvas.

CAVE 2: 6th century

This was a place of worship but since it is not of the usual pattern of a Buddhist chaitya, perhaps the form was borrowed from Brahmanical temples. The front of this cave is

Buddha stupa wide view

destroyed. On either side of the doorway is a tall 'dvarapala' standing on a lotus flower and a five hooded 'naga'. The figure on the left is Padmapani and the other figure is Indra. A Buddha seated on a 'simhasana' is inside the shrine attended by 'chauri' bearers and a circumambulatory path or 'pradakshinapatha' goes around.

CAVE 3: 5th century

This is the largest vihara of the first group. It consists of a columned verandah of approximately 9.5 metres with end chambers, a richly carved and columned hall with a central portico, cells at either side and an antechamber leading to a sanctuary at

Exterior view of Cave No. 7 of Aurangabad Caves

the back. The shrine is entered through an elaborate doorway. The interior presents a splendid tableau of kneeling devotees some with folded hands others with floral offerings gazing fervently towards the saviour. The figures have almost an Egyptian cast of countenance, with thick lips, very elaborate head dress and necklaces. Buddha sits in a preaching attitude and is attended by bejeweled Bodhisattvas.

CAVE 4: 1st century B.C.

Scholars differ as to the date of its excavation which ranges from the 2nd century B.C. to perhaps, the 4th century. It is a rectangular chaitya hall of great simplicity, containing a monolithic stupa partly preserved. The ceiling has finely carved ribs.

Between caves 4 and 5 is a rock-cut majestic image of Buddha flanked by Bodhisattvas seated on a lion throne.

CAVE 5: 6th century

This cave was probably a very small vihara now with the whole front gone. What remains is a very small shrine and circumambulatory path or 'pradakshinapatha' as well as traces of a hall or mandapa. Within the shrine is an image of the Buddha in 'padmanasana' with his hands in a dhyana mudra. This Buddha is comparable with some of the finest of the period.

Second Group or Northern Caves

CAVE 6: 6th century

This cave is a combination of a chaitya and a vihara. In the surrounding passageways are small shrines and those at rear corners have Buddha images. Finely carved Bodhisattva figures with attendants and flying celestials appear on either side of the sanctuary doorway. There is a colossal Buddha in teaching mode accompanied by kneeling devotees. Some fragments of painting survive on the ceiling of the verandah.

CAVE 7: 6th century

This is the finest cave of the second group and perhaps, the date of excavation can also be the seventh century. The plan of this cave is closer to Brahmanical temples. The sculptures are a Mahayana mythology and relate principally to Padmapani or Avalokitesvara. A panel of six goddesses are at the front of the shrine. Images of 'Hariti' and 'Panchika' are flanked by two female chauri bearers in sensuous stances.

Mandapa wall of Cave No. 7 of Aurangabad Caves

There is Manjushri in a very rich head-dress similar to those of the women of the island of Bali, and there is also Saraswati. The inner shrine has a circumambulatory passage or 'pradakshina-path' and a large Buddha in a preaching mode. The side walls have seated Buddhas accompanied by Lochana and Tara holding a lotus in one hand, a female dancer and female musicians.

CAVE 8

This is an unfinished cave.

CAVE 9: 6th century

This cave is very much ruined and the whole front has fallen.
There are other caves in the same hills belonging to the second and third group which lie unfinished. Cave 10, Cave 11 and Cave 12 are all in a plain and rough state.

DIVERSIONS IN AND AROUND AURANGABAD

ANWA TEMPLE

In the village of Anwa, on the road leading to the Ajanta caves approximately 90 kms from Aurangabad, is this temple dedicated to Lord Shiva. It was built by the Yadavas during the 12th century and consists of a sanctuary, a 'mandapa' or open hall and beautifully decorated pillars. The niches in the temple have exquisitely decorated sculpted images of Vishnu, Ganesha and other deities.

GAUTALA

About 72 kilometres from Aurangabad is a hilly terrain, wherein lies a sanctuary named after a well known ancient ascetic known as Gautam Rishi. There is a small cave which was his abode and many Rishis's or holy sages meditated here. The spot is very scenic as there are waterfalls, and lakes, dense vegetation and jungles. The Gautala sanctuary is spread over 260 km and has over two hundred species of birds. There are a variety of wild animals like leopards, deer, wolves, jackals, etc.

GRISHNESHWAR TEMPLE

This temple is situated in the village of Verul about half a mile from the Ellora caves and approximately 30 km from Aurangabad.

It was built by Rani Ahilyabai Holkar who ruled Indore from 1765 to 1795. She was a pious and philanthropic queen who constructed many religious structures accross the country.

Anwa Temple

The temple is dedicated to Lord Shiva and is the abode of one of the twelve Jyotirlinga shrines, considered as one of the most sacred places of worship. The temple also has a 'kund' or square tank, with a flight of steps descending to the water. The temple is a very good example of the modern style with the only visible Muslim influence in the crowning dome. A band of petals surrounds it below resembling other forms of Muslim domes in the Deccan. The entrance to the temple is through a small gate after which one enters an open courtyard. A moulded architrave leads to the inner shrine where a highly polished 'linga' of black stone is set in a moulded altar occupying the centre of the floor. The walls of the shrine have recesses for lamps. There is a larger recess at the back wall for an image, a passage leading from the antechamber to the shrine.

The temple is run by a trust of Brahmins who also conduct the daily rituals. Every year, in the month of March on Mahashivratri day, a huge fair is held here. Thousands of devotees flock to offer their prayers and get 'darshan'.

LONAR CRATER

This crater is approximately 165 kms from Aurangabad in the village of Lonar. It was formed by a meteorite impact nearly 30,000 years ago. The crater is 1830 metres across and nearly 150 metres deep. The rim is about 20 metres. It is the only known example on the earth of an impact crater in basalt rock. There is also a huge lake with blackish water with no outlet for the water from the crater. This stunning lake has an interesting range of acquatic birds, flora and fauna not found easily in other places.

A number of archaeological sites and temples exist in the area. Few images of Lord Vishnu and Brahma can be found as well. The area is being extensively developed and promoted as an eco-tourism spot.

NANDED

About 250 km away is the town of Nanded, on the banks of the serene and peaceful Godavari river, in the heart of the Marathwada region of Maharashtra.

Nanded is home to a dozen Gurudwaras, several of these are historic. Nanded, historians believe that it was visited by both the first and last Sikh Gurus, Guru Nanak and Guru Gobind Singh. The tenth Guru Gobind Singh (1666–1708) came to Nanded to seek Maratha support to fight the Mughal Empire under Emperor Aurangzeb. He made Nanded his permanent abode. Nanded, like Amritsar, is to the Sikhs what Mecca is to the Muslims, the Vatican to the Catholics and Kashi to the Hindus. It was here, exactly three centuries ago in 1708 that the world's youngest religion, Sikhism saw its tenth and last mortal master, Guru Gobind Singh consecrate the holy scripture, the Guru Granth Sahib, as the eternal Guru. This elevation of the Guru Granth Sahib is called 'Guru-ta-Gaddi'.

The Shri Huzur Sahib Abchal-nagar Sachkhand Gurudwara was constructed by Maharaja Ranjit Singh in 1837. The place where the Gurudwara stands today is said to be the spot where the hand written copy of the Granth Sahib was consecrated. The original copy went missing but another handwritten copy is still safe in the Gurudwara.

The armour and weapons used by Guru Gobind Singh are also on display. Today, modern day Nanded has seen fast and quick development especially in 2008, the 300th year of celebration of 'Guru-ta-Gaddi divas'. This tercentenary has been an important event in more ways than one. The press run by the Gurudwara Board announced: 'For the first 100 years, we were fighting the Mughals; the following 100 years we fought the British. This is the first time the third centenary is being celebrated in free India'.

PAITHAN

The town of Paithan is situated on the banks of the Godavari river at a distance of approximately 50 km from Aurangabad. This ancient town features in sacred Hindu literature under the name of 'Prathishtan', a Sanskrit word signifying 'the celestial abode of the gods'.

The history of Paithan can be traced to the powerful Satavahana dynasty in the 2nd century as it was their capital. This prosperous dynasty had established trade links with Rome.

Rich gold and silver brocades, tissues, other textiles, ivory products, conch bangles, ornaments made of terracotta and precious and semi precious stones were all produced in Paithan.

After the Satavahanas, came the Vakatakas followed by the Rashtrakutas and then the Yadavas. During the reign of the last two dynasties, Paithan grew in importance as a religious, cultural and spiritual centre particularly propagating the Bhakti cult. The Mughals followed and under their supremacy many mosques were built.

Present day Paithan occupies a very small portion of this ancient city. A wall now mostly in ruins, consisting of nine gateways surrounds the town. Principal places of interest are some ruins of the old fortress, remains of the Satavahana palace converted

A hand-woven Paithani saree in black and gold in a showroom

into a mosque and a shrine on the river bank, built in memory of a great religious leaded Eknath. There are numerous other temples dedicated to Shiva and some masjids scattered around.

Modern-day Paithan has assumed importance due to the construction of the Jayakwadi dam on the river Godavari. A well planned garden is artistically laid out with a variety of trees, plants, shrubs and flowers. It is named after Sant Dnyaneshwar.

At present, Paithan is the headquarters of the Tahsildar. It has a major post office and two government schools.

Paithan's Population consists traditionally of weavers and they continue to produce, however slowly, rich woven silk and cotton fabrics. The Paithani saree has a

An artisan weaving at the loom a Paithani Saree

very rich weave of gold and silver and it is six yards in length. It forms an important and expensive part of a Maharashtrian bride's trousseau.

PITALKHORA CAVES

Approximately 75 km from Aurangabad are the Pitalkhora caves. These thirteen caves are situated near a narrow ravine carved into the rock of the Satmala range of hills. The caves are in a ruined condition but they portray a period of great art, architecture, sculpture and heritage. There are invaluable inscriptions in the Brahmi script on the doorways and pillars pointing to the period of Emperor Ashoka. Sculptures of 'yakshas', 'mithunas', elephants, deer, horse and lions abound.

SHIRDI

This is a famous pilgrimage centre drawing devotees from around the world. It is believed that a mystic saint, who later came to be known as Sai Baba had miraculous healing powers. These powers originated in the form of a grey ash-like substance which emanated from a fire pit in his ashram. This potent ash became known as 'Vibhuti'. When this ash is applied to the human body it is believed to cure many ailments. Thursdays are special days of worship and the crowd of faithful devotees is huge. Since lines are long on Thursdays it would be best for visitors to select another day if the schedule permits.

HERITAGE WALKS

A renowned art historian couple Mr Rajat Qureshi and Mrs Dulari Qureshi have begun a programme of 'Heritage Walks'. These walks began from 2014 and are forty in number so far. They enlighten and educate the people of this city and other tourists about the illustrious history of Aurangabad.

SHOPPING AROUND

TEXTILES

Aurangabad is famous for its fabrics and textiles of silk and cotton, better known as 'Himroo', and another fabric called 'Mushroo'. Himroo is said to have originated in Persia and the designs are very Mughal. The manufacturing of Mushroo involves the famous 'tie and dye' technique, also well known in Rajasthan. Both fabrics are very durable, wash well and the colours are generally fast. They make interesting bedspreads, shawls and other items.

BIDRIWARE

These are very interesting articles of great beauty from Bidar, dating back to the Bahamani dynasty. These items are made either of steel or copper or an alloy of zinc and copper wherein gold or silver is inlaid onto the base metal. The process consists of five stages namely: casting, polishing, engraving, laying and lastly blackening the base metal. The range of articles is extensive: boxes, candle-sticks, goblets, jugs, vases, hookahs, cigarette boxes, ash-trays, cuff-links, etc.

JEWELLERY

The rocks and hills of Aurangabad are rich in deposits of natural mineral and stones. There is an abundance of semiprecious stones namely: agate, quartz, amethyst, bloodstone, black onyx, green onyx, malacite and many others.

An artisan weaving at the loom a Himroo fabric

Some of these coloured stones are in bead form; others in regular or irregular shapes. They are strung into necklaces of various lengths.

KITSCH SOUVENIRS

Inexpensive gifts to take back home are available all over the city. They are articles made of wood, lime stone or brass with coloured enamel inlay.

GLOSSARY

Abhaya mudra	hand position denoting protection; be not afraid
Abhishekha	the sprinkling of water for purification of an icon; a sacred image; consecration
Agni	Vedic fire divinity
Andhakasura	demon killed by Shiva
Apasmara purusha	the dwarf demon crushed by Lord Shiva under his foot during the cosmic dance - Tandava
Apsaras	celestial maidens or beautiful courtesans of the gods
Ardhanarishvara	Lord who is half man and half woman
Arjuna	important hero of Mahabharata to whom Krishna recited the Bhagvad Gita
Avalokitesvara	the Buddha of Compassion
Avatar	incarnation of a god manifested in a physical form especially pertaining to Lord Vishnu
Balarama	Subhadra's brother, also elder brother of Krishna
Bhakti	Intense devotion to an incarnated deity
Bhikshu's	Buddhist monks
Bibi	Mother
Bodhi	the ficus tree under which Buddha gained enlightenment
Bodhisattva	those beings who are on the threshold of enlightenment or a potential Buddha to be
Brahma	the creator and a God recognized by four heads
Buddha	'The Enlightened One' the title was given to Gautama who propagated a path of simple ethical living known as Buddhism. The Buddha was soon worshipped as a God
Chaitya	structure meant for worship of the stupa, apsidal in form with serialized columns and having a vaulted roof
Chaitya-griha	a prayer hall containing a stupa
Chalukyas	early Chalukyas 6th-8th century a dynasty of the Deccan
Chamunda or Chunda	a multi armed goddess created by Durga to destroy evil
Char-bagh	a garden divided into four parts by four water channels which meet in the centre

Chauri bearers	fan bearers; an attendant to an important personage or God
Chausar	a game played with dice
Chhatri	a cenotaph of the Rajputs; an umbrella shaped dome or pavilion
Chintamani	a wish full-filling jewel
Dakhni	the local people of the Deccan
Damaru	a small hour glass shaped drum identified with Lord Shiva.
Dargah	(Persian) a holy place of pilgrimage containing the remains of Sufi saints
Darshan	the act of viewing an enshrined diety
Darul Islam	land of light and peace
Darwaza	gate
Devi	goddess
Dharini	concept reduced to a single seed syllable
Dharma	the law; moral doctrine taught by the Buddha
Dharmachakra-Pravartana mudra	hand gesture of Buddha, denoting turning of the wheel of law
Dhyana	meditation
Dhyana mudra	a gesture of meditation where the hands rest upon Buddha's lap one above the other palms facing upwards
Dhyani Buddhas	Bodhisattavas of the first order
Dikpalas	door guardians indicating the four directions
Durga	principal Goddess of the Shakti cult riding on a lion or tiger destroying a buffalo demon
Finial	a crowning ornament on a spire
Gaja - Lakshmi	Goddess of victory always shown lustrated by elephants
Gana	dwarf-like playful creature; attendants of Lord Shiva
Gandharvas	semi-divine male flying figures
Ganesh	Elephant headed God of good beginnings and invoked at the start of any new undertaking
Ganga	goddess personifying the Ganga river
Ghata	vase motif in sculpture
Ghata - Pallava	vase and foliage capitals characteristic of Gupta period
Gomateshvara	also known as Bahubali sometimes regarded as a Tirthankara
Gopura or Gopuram	tall pyramidal gate of a South Indian temple
Grishneshwara	name of Shiva worshipped at temple of same name near Ellora

Gupta	during the reign of the Gupta dynasty from 320–647 literature, art, mathematics and astronomy reached great heights. The Gupta period Buddha image became the model for artists across the Buddhist world
Guru	teacher or a learned man
Hariti	Goddess of prosperity and patroness of children
Harmika	pavilion, railed balcony surmounting the dome of the stupa
Hinayana	the "lesser vehicle" referring to Theravada Buddhism
Indra	king of the gods and lord of the heavens and storms
Iwan	vaulted hall in a Mosque
Jainism	a religious faith founded by Lord Mahavira
Jama Masjid	A congregational Mosque
Jambhala	God of riches
Jataka	Tales or stories concerning the former lives of Buddha
Jina	conqueror
Jnanketu	a Bodhisattva sometimes with a flower stalk in his left hand and sometimes holding a pennan
Juma	Friday when Muslims congregate to say special prayers at the mosque
Kacheri	court
Kailasha	Lord Shiva's abode in the Himalayas
Kalachuri	a dynasty that rules the western region during the 6th century and was responsible for initiating rock-cut Hindu architecture
Kalasha	a pot like finial
Karma	fate; power to influence the future of an individual, either for good or bad; all phenomena result from a cause, and action is followed by its effect.
Kartikeya	warrior son of Shiva and Parvati
Killa	Fort or palace
Krishna	incarnation of Vishnu; also the popular divinity who appears as Govinda and the Charioteer of Arjuna in the Mahabharata
Kubera	Chief of the Yakshas; pot-bellied keeper of the earths treasures
Lakshmi	Goddess of wealth
Lena - lene	rock cut cave
Linga	Shiva-linga or phallus; the object of worship within the sanctum of a Shiva temple
Machicolated	projecting parapet carried on brackets
Madrassa	a school for the teaching of Islam that includes both lecture halls and residential accommodation for students

Mahabharata	Great Indian Epic that narrates the great war that took place between the Pandavas and the Kaurava clan.
Mahal	palace
Mahamayuri	is a Buddhist goddess identified with a peacock and is a consort of Amoghasiddhi Bodhisattva
Mahapratiharya	great miracle of the Buddha at Shravasti
Mahayana	"Greater Vehicle" major philosophal principles which were the later aspects of Buddhism
Mahishasura	buffalo demon slain by Durga
Mahosadha	wise hero of a Jataka story
Maitreya	benevolent Buddha and Buddha of the future
Makaras	a water creature, part fish or crocodile with an elephant type head
Makbara	tomb; grave
Mandala	a square or circular cosmic diagram, symbol of the universe, used as a vehicle for meditation and ritual
Mandapa	the hall of a temple or shrine
Manjushri	Bodhisattva whose special duty is to stimulate understanding, sometimes holds a sword to destroy falsehood
Manushi	seven mortal Buddhas name of a series of earthly saviours
Mara	the evil one in Buddhism who tempted the Buddha and tried to prevent him from enlightenment
Masjid	Arabic word for mosque; literally 'a place for prostration'
Matysa	fish and the first incarnation of Lord Vishnu
Maurya	the first Indian empire founded by Chandragupta Maurya, Emperor Ashoka who ruled during C. 272-31 sponsored the first monumental art in stone in his columns with edicts of Buddhism as well as the first rock - cut caves
Merlon	parapet battlements with pointed tops
Mihrab	an alcove or niche in a mosque that indicates the direction of Mecca towards which Muslims must face when saying their prayers
Minaret	A tower attached to a mosque from which the faithful are called to prayer five times a day
Mithuna	loving couple; emblems of fertility
Mudra	symbolic hand gesture signifying various actions
Nagas	serpent community Inhabiting a watery kingdom in the Patala region underneath the earth; they have great influence and are worshipped in

	their own right; they were absorbed into Buddhism as supporters and protectors
Naga-raja	serpent king
Nandi	bull mount of Shiva
Naqarkhana	a music hall
Narsimha	incarnation of Vishnu as a man-lion
Nataraj	Lord of Dance and generally refers to Lord Shiva Naubat Music
Nilakantha	blue throated; epithet of Shiva after he drank the poison produced at the churning of the cosmic ocean
Nirvana	enlightenment
Padmapani	Bodhisattva epithet of Avalokiteshvara distinguished by the lotus flower he holds
Pairidaeza	(Persian) walled garden; paradise
Panchika	Wealth God; another name for Kubera
Parinirvana	The Great Nirvana; Buddha leaving the world; his physical death
Parshvanath	the second last of the twenty four Tirthankaras
Parvati	daughter of the mountain and consort of Shiva
Pradakshina	the ritual of the circumambulatory path or going around a sacred image in a clockwise direction
Pradakshinapatha	the ritual of the circumambulatory path or going around a sacred image in a clockwise direction
Puranas	old sacred literature compiled during the first millennium that are compilations of traditional lore
Qibla	The wall of a mosque marking the direction to face Mecca, this wall is in the West
Qilla	Palace or fort
Rajputs	dynasties of western and central India from 14th–20th centuries
Ramayana	A Great Indian Epic, "the story of Rama' tells the tale of the exile of Rama, prince of Ayodhya, together with his wife Sita and brother Lakshmana
Rashtrakuta	a 7th–10th century dynasty of the Deccan
Ravana	demon king of Sri Lanka and slain by Rama in the Ramayana
Saivism	pertaining to the cult of Shiva
Sala-bhanjika	a female who touches a tree to make it grow; a sculpture motif; a fertility symbol

Samsara	circle of rebirths or eternal transmigration of the soul
Sapta matrikas	seven mothers who are worshipped as deities in a group
Sarai	a resting place for weary travelers
Satavahana	Hindu dynasty of the Deccan ruled from 757–783 and responsible for the rock-cut monolithic Kailashnatha at Ellora
Shakti	female energy and power associated with the goddess
Shikhara	or mountain peak, the spire of a Hindu, Jain or Buddhist temple
Shiva	Lord Shiva is a major Hindu god carrying a trident
Simhasana	lion throne
Sthirachakra	Bodhisattva holding a sword
Stucco	plasterwork
Stupa	a solid earthern memorial mound enshrining a relic casket containing the remains of the Buddha or venerated Buddhist teachers
Stylobate	a platform on which stands a colonnade
Subhadra	sister of Krishna and wife of Arjuna
Sufi	a mystic saint generally of Islamic tradition
Sujata's offering	maiden who offered rice to Buddha after his enlightenment of pyasa
Sultanate	a term given to Muslim Turkish rule under five separate dynasties: Slave, Khilji, Tughlak, Sayyid and Lodi. In the Deccan the Bahmani Sultanate was in power from 1347–1538
Tandava	the dance associated with Lord Shiva
Tantra	a later development in Buddhism focusing on female and male polarity and their relative dependence; a body of literature
Tantrikas	those who adhere to tantric practices
Tara	Star : a Goddess known in Hindu, Jain and Buddhist religion
Theravada	orthodox school of Buddhism
Tirthankara	a Jain founder or conqueror and there are 24 such beings in the Jain religion
Todar Mal	There is no name in mediaeval history more renowned in India than Raja Todarmal who was the famous Minister of Revenue in the court of Mughal Emperor Akbar
Tri-kaya	the three bodies or three fold nature of the Buddhist doctrine
Trivikrama	incarnation of Vishnu pacing out the universe in three gigantic strides
Tawarikh-Nama	a chronicle or history of dates and events
Upanishads	a body of ancient philosophical, poetic literature primarily considered a part of the Vedas

Urs	'Wedding', a death anniversary of a saint commemorated as one whose soul has been 'wedded' to God
Vaishnavism	pertaining to the cult of the vedas
Vajra	diamond scepter or thunderbolt
Vajra Paryankasana	Buddha in a preaching pose
Vajrapani	Bodhisattva holding the thunderbolt
Vakataka	a 4th - 5th century dynasty of the Deccan
Vaman	dwarf incarnation of Vishnu
Vamanika	female dwarf
Varada mudra	a hand gesture where the hand is stretched downwards denoting charity
Varuna	Vedic god of the waters and guardian of the west shown with a makara
Vayu	Vedic god of air and guardian of the north-west
Vedas	oldest and earliest known religious, Brahmanical texts
Vidyadharas	flying figures
Viharas	Buddhist monastries with accommodation for monks living in communities
Vishnu	This God is distinguished by the war discus and conch shell trumpet that he holds, and Lord Vishnu wears a tall crown
Vishvakarma	mythical architect of the heavens
Vyakhyana mudra	in Buddhist texts interchangeable with dharmachakra-pravartana mudra
Yakshas/Yakshi	gods and goddesses of fertility
Yadavas	a dynasty of Deogiri Deccan, or the present day Daulatabad, whose ruler Bhillama founder the city of Deogiri around 1192 A.D.
Yama	god of death
Yamuna	goddess personifying the Yamuna river
Zenana	segregated women's quarters

REFERENCES

Introduction:
Joshi Rekha, 1979, Aurangzeb - Attitudes and Inclinations, Pg 27
Sarkar J. N., 1964 History of Aurangzeb, Vol III, Pg 163 - 164
Dehejia Vidya, 1997, Indian Art, Pg 267
Gazetteer of Aurangabad District 1884, Pg 117

Walled City:
Gazetteer of Aurangabad District 1884, Pg 597
Davies Phillip, 1989, Monuments of India Vol. ll, Pg 61
Gazetteer of Aurangabad District 1884. Pg 595
Davies Phillip, 1989, Monuments of India Vol. ll, Pg 29
Gascoigne Bamber, 1971, The Great Moghuls, Pg 222
Davies Phillip, 1989, Monuments of India Vol. ll, Pg 451
Davies Phillip, 1989, Monuments of India Vol. ll, Pg 452

Rock - Cut Cave Architecture:
Basham A. L., 1963, The Wonder that was India, Pg 346 - 379

Ajanta Caves:
Grousset Reus, The Civilizations of the East - India, Pg 44 - 156
Sastri Nilakanta K.A., 1952, Benares, Age of Nandas & Mauryas, Pg 390
Khandalavala Karl, 1974, "The Development of Style in India Painting" (Bombay Heras Institute, Heras Memorial Lecture)
Craven Roy C., 1976, Indian Art - A concise history, Pg 127
Gazetteer of Aurangabad District, 1884, Pg 436
(Dr Bhau Daji in J.R.A.S. Bombay Branch Vol. Vll and also Mr John Griffith's as quoted in the Kandosh Gazetteer)
Majumdar R.C., 1951 London, The Vedic Age, Pg 146 - 147
Huntingdon Susan L, 1985, The Art of Ancient India, Pg 259 - 260
Gazetteer of Aurangabad District 1884, Pg 436
Michell George, 1989, Monuments of India Vol. l, Pg 335 - 336

Ellora Caves:
Ramaswami. N. S., quotes Capt. John Seely in his book "Indian Monuments" Pg 62 - 63 printed in a paper called "Indian Sculpture, The scene, Themes and Legends", by Randhawa Mohinder Singh and Randhawa Doris S., 1985, Vakils, Feffer & Simons Ltd., Chapter XlV on Rashtrakutas, Ellora Sixth - Eighth Centuries A.D.
Dhavalikar Prof. M.K., 2003, 'Ellora-Monumental Legacy', Pg 20-39

Aurangabad Caves:
Berkson Carmel, 1986, The caves at Aurangabad, (Early Buddhist & Tantric Art in India), Pg 29
Burgess - Report of the Antiquities in the Bidar and Aurangabad Districts 1875, London 1875, Pg 81
Huntingdon Susan L., 1985, The Art of Ancient India, Pg 266 – 268

BIBLIOGRAPHY

1. Ali Athar M. 1966, The Mughal Nobility under Aurangzeb, Aligarh University, Oxford University Press, New Delhi
2. Basham A. L., 1963, The Wonder that was India, Rupa & Co., New Delhi
3. Berkson Carmel, 1986, The caves at Aurangabad, (Early Buddhist & Tantric Art in India), Mapin Publishing, New York
4. Bernier Francois, 1934, Travels in the Moghul Empire (translated by Archibald Constable) D.K. Fine Art Press Pvt. Ltd., New Delhi
5. Craven Roy C., 1976, Indian Art - A concise history, Thames & Hudson, London
6. Davies Phillip, 1989 Monuments of India Vol. ll, Penguin Group, England
7. Dehejia Vidya, 1997, Indian Art, Phaidon Press Ltd. London
8. Dhavalikar Prof. M.K., 2003, Ellora - Monumental Legacy, Oxford University Press, New Delhi
9. Elgood Heather, 2000, Hinduism & the Religious Arts, Cassel Publishing, London/New York
10. Festing Gabrielle, 1997, When Kings rode to Delhi, Asian Educational Services, New Delhi
11. Gascoigne Bamber, 1971, The Great Moghuls, Jonathan Cape Ltd., 30 Bedford Square, London WC1
12. Gazetteer of Aurangabad District originally printed in 1884 (Gazetteers Dept., Govt. of Maharashtra)
13. Grousset Reus, The Civilizations of the East, India
14. Holden Edward S., 2004, The Moghul Emperors of Hindustan, Asian Educational Services, Delhi
15. Huntingdon Susan L, 1985, The Art of Ancient India, Weatherhill, New York
16. Irvine William, 1991, A translation of 'A Pepys of Moghul India; an abridged edition of the 'Storia Do Mogor' of Niccolao Manucci, Asian Educational Services, New Delhi
17. Joshi Rekha, 1979 Aurangzeb - Attitudes and Inclinations, Munshiram, Manaharlal Publishers Pvt. Ltd., New Delhi
18. Joshi R. M., 1956, Poona Akhbars, Vol. lll, Central Records Office, Govt of Andhra Pradesh Hyderabad
19. Khandalavala Karl, 1991, 'The Golden Age', Marg Publications, Mumbai
20. Majumdar R.C., 1951, The Vedic Age, London
21. Michell George, 1989, Monuments of India Vol. l, Penguin Group, England

22. Mitra Debala, 1992, Ajanta – A publication of Archaelogical Survey of India, New Delhi
23. Moreland W. H., 1923, From Akbar to Aurangzeb, Low Price Publications, Delhi
24. Okada Amina, 1992, Indian Miniatures of the Mughal Court, Harry N Abrams Inc., New York
25. Poole Lane Stanley, 1990, Aurangzeb and the Decay of the Mughal Empire, Low Price Publications, Delhi
26. Prasad Ishwari, 1968, A New History of India, The Indian Press Pvt. Ltd., Allahabad
27. Pushpesh Pant, Ajanta & Ellora
28. Qureshi Gupte Dulari, 1999, Tourism Potential in Aurangabad, Bhartiya Kala Prakashan Delhi
29. Qureshi Gupte Dulari & Qureshi Rafat Dr, Aurangabad Nama—A History of Aurangabad
30. Ramaswami N.S., "Indian Monuments in Indian Sculpture, The Scene,Themes & Legends"
31 Randhawa Mohinder Singh and Randhawa Doris S., 1985, Chapter XlV on Rashtrakutas, Ellora Sixth - Eighth Centuries A.D., Vakils, Feffer & Simons Ltd.
32. Report of the Antiquities in the Bidar and Aurangabad Districts 1875, London
33. Sarkar J.N. 1964, The Fall of the Mughal Empire, Vol. l - lV, Orient Longman, Delhi
34. Sarkar J. N. 1989, 'Studies in Aurangzeb's Reign', Sangam Books, Calcutta
35. Sastri Nilakanta K.A., 1952, 'Age of Nandas & Mauryas', Benares
36. Schimmel Annemarie, 2004, The Empire of the Great Mughals, Reaktion Books Ltd., London
37. Singh Asa, 1966-67, the Sikh Review Vol. 14 - 16, Sikh Cultural Centre, Calcutta
38. Singh Madanjeet, 1965, Ajanta, (Edita Lausanne specially printed for Air India), Switzerland.
39. Sitapati Sri P. 1980, Farmans and Sanads of the Deccan Sultans, State Archives, Govt. of Andhra Pradesh, Hyderabad
40. Spear Percival, 1961, India, University of Michigan Press Ann- Arbor
41. Tavernier Jean Baptisite, 2000, (translated by V. Ball), D.K. Fine Art Press, Delhi
42. Thapar Romila, 2003, The Penguin History of Early India (From the origins to A.D. 1300, Penguins Books)
43. Yazdani G. and Others, 1930 - 1955, Ajanta Parts l - lV, Oxford
44. Yazdani G., 1960, The Early History of the Deccan, Parts l - Vl, Oxford

ACKNOWLEDGEMENT

Last but not the least, grateful thanks to my husband Arvind who has always supported my endeavours.

PHOTOGRAPHIC ACKNOWLEDGEMENTS

1) Mr Benoy K Behl - For Ajanta Caves
2) Mr Purshotam Deshpande - Professional Photographer in Aurangabad
3) Dr Rafat Qureshi & Dulari Qureshi - Photo of Malik Amber

ABOUT THE AUTHOR

Mrs Rashmi Jolly has over forty years of experience as an Executive Director overseeing the public relations and export activities of the Jolly Group of Companies, Mumbai. She is now Vice-Chairperson and Executive Director of Jollyboard Ltd. An Honorary Consul of the Czech Republic for Mumbai, Maharashtra and Goa, she has been promoting Czech art, culture, fashion and music for the past ten years. An English literature graduate from Lady Shriram College, University of Delhi, Jolly has done her Post Graduate Diploma in Asian Art from the British Museum, London. As an avid collector of contemporary Indian art for over forty years, she has been published several times in the *Times of India* and other leading publications. A keen environmentalist, Mrs Jolly is also known to encourage and promote young and upcoming artists.

QUEEN ELIZABETH II in Exeter

Her Majesty The Queen and Prince Philip at the corner of Bedford Street and Princesshay, 2 May 1956.

QUEEN ELIZABETH II in Exeter

Todd Gray

The Mint Press Exeter

First published 2022

A publication of The Mint Press
Taddyforde House South
Taddyforde Estate
New North Road, Exeter EX4 4AT

website: www.stevensbooks.co.uk
tel: 01392 459760
email: sales@themintpress.co.uk

ISBN 978 1903 356 78 4

A CIP catalogue record for this book is available from the British Library
The publisher has no responsibility for the continued existence or accuracy of URLs for external or third-party internet websites referred to in this book, and does not guarantee that any content on such websites is, or will remain, accurate or appropriate.
This publication is printed on acid-free paper

Typeset, printed and bound by Short Run Press, Exeter

Contents

Acknowledgements

I would like to thank Reg Erskine, Richard Lappas, Mark Rothwell and Alan Quick (*Crediton Courier*), Simon Kitchen & Rosalie Robison (Devon County Council), John Street, Steve Stewart & Emara Roth (Exeter City Council), Nicholas Warren (*Express & Echo*), Carey MacKenzie (Step One Charity) and Dr Christine Faunch & Kerra Maddern (University of Exeter). The illustrations appear courtesy of Step One Charity (1, 14, 31), *Express & Echo* (2-4, 6, 8, 14, 18, 20, 22, 27, 33), Exeter City Council (5, 7, 9-10, 12-13, 15, 17, 19, 21, 23-6, 28-30, 34-42, 45), Special Collections, University of Exeter (11 {EUL UA/P/3e}), Devon County Council (16), Alan Quick of the *Crediton Courier* (28), Richard Lappas (32) and University of Exeter (43-4).

Dedicated to the memory of David Herbert, Exeter Freeman

Foreword

Queen Elizabeth II visited Exeter on eleven occasions. On each visit she expressed that keen and earnest devotion to a life of public service which we all associate with her extraordinarily long reign. The people of Exeter consistently gave her a warm and enthusiastic reception. Her Majesty inaugurated our rebuilding after the Second World War and checked up on us in the following eight decades. We are still mourning her passing but I am confident that these images will help us remember how fortunate we were in having a sovereign who gave such exemplary service. While we look forward to a bright future under His Majesty the King, we can also cherish these visual reminders of the past.

I warmly recommend this book,

Councillor Mrs Yolonda Henson, *Lord Mayor of Exeter*

Corporate Sponsor

Princesshay

Individual Patrons

John Ambacher
Eleanor Beebe
Paul Harding
Sue & Pete Jackson
Claire & Mark Richardson
Ray & Alison Lawry

Introduction

'I can make my solemn act of dedication with a whole Empire listening. I should like to make that dedication now. It is very simple. I declare before you all that my whole life, whether it be long or short, shall be devoted to your service and to the service of our great imperial family to which we all belong. But I shall not have strength to carry out this resolution alone unless you join in it with me as I now invite you to do.' 21 April 1947

Elizabeth II, by the Grace of God, of the United Kingdom of Great Britain and Northern Ireland Queen, Head of the Commonwealth, Defender of the Faith, was born on 21 April 1926 in Mayfair. She was the first child of Prince Albert, Duke of York, and Lady Elizabeth Bowes-Lyon. In the private chapel at Buckingham Palace she was christened Elizabeth Alexandra Mary after her mother, her paternal great-grandmother, Queen Alexandra and paternal grandmother, Queen Mary. Upon the abdication in 1936 of her uncle, Edward VIII, she became heir presumptive. Her teenage years, during the war, were largely spent with her sister Margaret at Windsor Castle and on 20 November 1947 she married Lieutenant Philip Mountbatten RN, formerly Prince Philip of Greece and Denmark. Their first child, Prince Charles, was born in 1948 and he was followed by Anne (in 1950), Andrew (1960) and Edward (1964). Princess Elizabeth acceded to the throne on 6 February 1952 upon the death of her father, George VI, and on the 8th thousands of Exonians gathered in six locations across the city to hear her accession proclamation. The coronation took place on 2 June 1953.

Only six queens had ruled during the previous five hundred years. Lady Jane Grey was on the throne for a mere nine days and Anne, Mary I and Mary II each had reigns of five years, but Elizabeth I and Victoria ruled for 45 and 63 years. In comparison, Elizabeth II was on the throne longer than any British sovereign, male or female. She celebrated her Silver Jubilee in 1977, her Golden Jubilee in 2002, her Diamond Jubilee in 2012 and her Platinum Jubilee in 2022. She reigned for seventy years.

Her Royal Majesty died at Balmoral on 8

September 2022 and laid in state at St Giles Cathedral in Edinburgh and Westminster Abbey where she had married and been crowned. Her funeral took place on the 19th at Westminster Abbey and she was interred in a private ceremony that day at St George's Chapel in Windsor Castle.

No ruling monarch had visited Exeter so often. Her Majesty came on eleven occasions from 1946 to 2012 and these visits were commemorated by the naming of Princesshay (1949), Queen's Drive (1956) and Queen's Building (1956). In addition, in 1927, two decades before her first visit, the Princess Elizabeth Orthopaedic Hospital was named after her by her mother. One of her lasting commitments to Exeter was her patronage of St Loyes of some seventy-five years. It was in connection with that, that a week before her wedding in 1947, Princess Elizabeth attended the Flower Ball at the Savoy Hotel, a fundraiser for the college.[1]

Since 1497 every sovereign, on arriving in Exeter, has had the civic sword surrendered to her or him by the mayor. The guildhall, which houses the civic regalia, was visited by the Queen more often than any other building in Exeter. On six of her visits to Exeter Her Majesty arrived in the Royal Train but her transport has also involved motor cars, aeroplanes and, on one occasion, a helicopter. Prince Philip accompanied her on nearly every visit.

Princess Elizabeth saw Exeter in its ruined state in 1946, inaugurated its rebuilding in 1949 and as Queen, witnessed extraordinary change and growth through to her last visit in 2012. We will never know her private thoughts on how Exeter developed but her keen sense of duty increasingly ensured, with every visit, a warm and enthusiastic public reception. It may have been a mark of her regard for Exeter that in 2005 she personally sanctioned the temporary loan of the Exeter Salt to Exeter Guildhall, the first item ever to be loaned from the Crown Jewels and Plate.

1

13 & 14 November 1946

Her Royal Highness The Princess Elizabeth was twenty years old on her first visit. War had recently ended but the city centre remained in ruins following the blitz of 1942.

At 2.18 pm Princess Elizabeth arrived in a saloon coach of an ordinary train at St David's Station with the Hon. Mrs Andrew Elphinstone in attendance. Her Royal Highness wore a fitted, flared coat of deep turquoise with a matching off-the-face hat accompanied by a double row of pearls and a jewelled lapel brooch. She was greeted by Earl Fortescue, Lord Lieutenant, and Mayor W. O. Wills.

Some 7,000 children lined the route to the guildhall where she signed the Distinguished Visitors' Book. The royal car then travelled through the 'bombed but beflagged streets' to the Royal West of England Residential School for the Deaf where 130 children raised three cheers. The final stop was St Loyes College for the Training and Rehabilitation of the Disabled where Her Highness opened the new extension and said:

'I would like to take this opportunity of paying tribute to your courage and determination and to congratulate you on the remarkable results. I would like to say – you are needed, every one of you. Your skill, your fortitude, your industry are urgently required for a multitude of tasks. By showing these qualities you are setting a magnificent example to the rest of the community, so short of trained craftsmen and workers. I wish you all long life and happiness – happiness that comes from the sure knowledge that you are able to play your full part in helping the country and your fellow men'.

One newspaper was headlined 'Princess praises pluck of disabled'.

After staying overnight with the Fortescue family at Castle Hill Princess Elizabeth returned to Exeter. She wore a turquoise halo hat ruched with net. Her woollen coat was fawn-coloured, fitted tightly to the waist and flared into a wide skirt. The princess visited Topsham Barracks (renamed Wyvern Barracks in 1960) where she inspected a parade of service cadets and cadet units of the British Red Cross and the Order of St John. After lunch in the guildhall, Princess Elizabeth toured the orthopaedic hospital named after her in 1927. It was then said she 'showed a genius for chatting with patients on the topics which interested them most'. A common feature of the newspaper coverage was that the visit would be remembered in part for the 'complete lack of ostentation'.[2]

Princess Elizabeth laying a brick for the extension of the production shop at St Loyes College, 13 November 1946.

The Royal procession along the western end of High Street which had not suffered bombing in 1942, 14 November 1946.

Princess Elizabeth at the Princess Elizabeth Orthopaedic Hospital meeting Derek Robillard, occupant of the Princess Elizabeth Cot, 14 November 1946.

The inspection of cadets of the British Red Cross Society at Block 8, Topsham Barracks, 14 November 1946.

2

21 October 1949

Princess Elizabeth's second visit took place two years following her marriage to Philip, Duke of Edinburgh, and nearly a year since the birth of their first child, Prince Charles. Her official title was Her Royal Highness The Princess Elizabeth, Duchess of Edinburgh. The visit initiated the city's reconstruction. In attendance was Lady Alice Egerton.

Her Royal Highness was met at the city's boundary in Whipton by Mayor W. G. Michelmore who escorted her to the guildhall for lunch. She wore a long close-fitting coat of deep plum with a fan-shaped satin bow of pale blue at the neck and a small hat of the same shade of red ornamented with small blue feathers.

After lunch she fixed a bronze plaque for Princesshay, the pedestrian development built in the city centre and was given the silver screwdriver 'as a memento'. Her Royal Highness had consented to her name being used alongside the many ancient places named 'hays' such as Bonhay, Northernhay and Southernhay.

Some 10,000 people gathered in what a journalist described as 'the heart of the city where Hitler's bombers showered death and destruction from the night skies in May 1942'. Her Royal Highness spoke of having seen war damage three years earlier and commented:

'I saw enough then to realise how much you had lost in what were surely among the most senseless and unwarranted air raids that ever took place. If much that you loved and admired has been destroyed you have, by way of recompense, an opportunity which is given to few cities. In these crowded islands, we have little space to build and it is seldom that the men of the twentieth century have a chance to show what they can do in the very centre of a town. We are apt to criticise shapeless suburbs, which in some places have grown up without style or taste. But the centre of Exeter is something quite different, and what rises here will be an example by which the architecture and planning of our generation will be judged in years to come'.

The mayor pointed out Princesshay's alignment allowed views of the cathedral's two towers.

The remainder of the afternoon involved laying the foundation stone for Toronto House, in Stoke Hill, an inspection of council houses and her first visit to the cathedral where she viewed the reconstruction following war damage. The last event was tea in the mayor's parlour.[3]

Princess Elizabeth processing with Mayor Michelmore and preceded by two mace sergeants, 21 October 1949.

Workmen preparing for the arrival of Princess Elizabeth. High Street can be seen in the background.
This pedestrian shopping mall was demolished in 2005 and the second Princesshay opened in the autumn of 2007.

Princess Elizabeth inaugurating the rebuilding of Exeter following the Second World War, 21 October 1949.

The visit to Stoke Hill, 21 October 1949.

3

8 May 1956

Seven years later the Queen returned and commented 'It is nice to be back again. It is quite a long time since I was here'. It was the first visit to Exeter by a reigning queen. Only four years earlier she had acceded to the throne. At this time Her Majesty was having weekly audiences with her second prime minister, Sir Anthony Eden.

Mayor J. Greenslade met the royal couple at Cowley Bridge, the city's boundary, and the civic sword was surrendered as it would be on all subsequent visits. The first stop was the university where gowned undergraduates greeted Her Majesty who wore a fitted coat of silver grey stiffened silk, over a frock of the same colour with a matching hat of straw with a cerise ribbon and a rosette at the back. She presented the charter to Mary, Duchess of Devonshire who was the university Chancellor as well as Her Majesty's Mistress of the Robes. This was understood to be the first occasion on which a reigning monarch had personally given a charter. She said:

'This is the third university – Southampton and Hull being the others – to be founded in my reign. I think that this bears striking witness to the increase in the facilities for higher education which are being provided throughout the kingdom – a development which has its counterpart in the colonies and in the other countries of the Commonwealth… There is a great need in the world today for technical and scientific education but side by side with that it is important to maintain the study of the humanities, in which Britain has for centuries held an honoured name'.

The University College of the South West of England had been formed in the late 1800s with its degrees conferred by the University of London.

The Queen dropped a box containing a Coronation five shillings piece into the hollow of the foundation stone of the new humanities building which she named Queen's Building and consented to the naming of 'The Queen's Drive'. The royal couple also viewed the Exeter Poetry Book and Exeter Domesday at an exhibition organised by Audrey Erskine.

Afterwards the Royal Party lunched at the guildhall, toured the city and visited the King George V Playing Fields at Countess Wear. On its return to London the Royal Train stopped for seventeen minutes at Cowley Bridge Junction in order to admit the Queen's first cousin, Mrs Denys Rhodes of Tiverton, and her family.[4]

Her Majesty with Mary, Duchess of Devonshire, at the university, 2 May 1956.

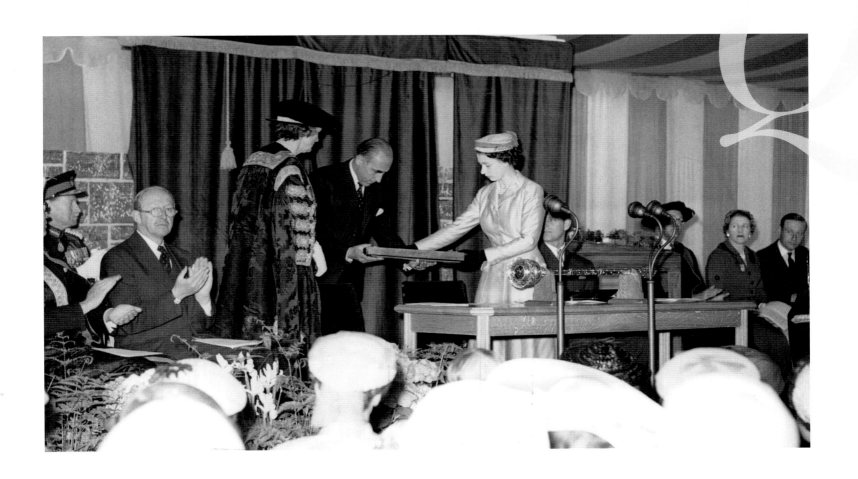

The Queen presenting the charter, 2 May 1956.

A rare early colour photograph of the Queen leaving the Mary Harris Memorial Chapel, University of Exeter, 2 May 1956.

The Queen and Prince Phillip at Countess Wear, 2 May 1956.

4

5 August 1977

Twenty-one years after her last visit Her Majesty came to Exeter during her Silver Jubilee, the twenty-fifth anniversary of her accession to the throne. She was then having weekly audiences with her seventh prime minister, James Callaghan. Thirteen years earlier, in 1964, Bobby's, the landmark building at the western end of Sidwell Street, had been built. In 1971 the Church of St Mary Major in Cathedral Close had been demolished and a Roman bathhouse was subsequently discovered in an archaeological excavation. Sir John Hannam, a Conservative, had been the city's Member of Parliament for seven years.

When the Queen and Prince Philip arrived there had already been extensive commemorations across the country. The royal couple disembarked from H. M Yacht *Britannia* in the Royal Barge at Torquay and were driven in their Rolls Royce to the city centre via Alphington Road, over the recently-built Exe Bridge and up Fore Street to the guildhall where Mayor Roger Keast surrendered the civic sword.

The royal couple travelled to County Hall where presentations were made on the terrace in front of Bellair, the early eighteenth-century house situated within the grounds. The general public and members of youth organisations were greeted in a circular walkabout through the grounds. Afterwards, there was lunch with the Samuel Sargent, Chairman of Devon County Counci, who presented Her Majesty with a bound volume entitled *Devonshire Illustrated in a Series of Views*. This was followed by an afternoon visit to Haldon Racecourse to witness the running of the Duchy Cup. The Queen and Prince Philip rode in the open carriage which was used at Ascot and it was pulled by the same grey horses. The Royal party then travelled on to Plymouth.

A month later a bronze sculpture, entitled 'Looking Forward' was unveiled behind the guildhall in the Guildhall Shopping Centre in Exeter. It commemorated the Silver Jubilee.[5]

Mayor Keast surrendering the sword, 5 August 1977.

27

The Queen at the guildhall, 5 August 1977.

The Queen at Bellair House, Devon County Hall, 5 August 1977.

The Queen on a walkabout at County Hall, 5 August 1977.

5

9 November 1979

It was only two years later that Her Majesty returned for a six-hour visit. At this time she was having weekly audiences with her eighth prime minister, Mrs Margaret Thatcher. The Guildhall Shopping Centre had only recently been built.

The Royal Train pulled into St David's Station in the morning and the Queen and the Duke of Edinburgh were received by Field Marshall Sir Richard Hull, Lord Lieutenant, and Mayor Richard van Oppen. Her Majesty wore a red coat and black hat with a red cockade.

As in 1946, the Queen visited St Loyes College, of which Her Majesty was Patron, opened Northcott House and then travelled through Burnthouse Lane, Dryden Lane and Barrack Road to the Princess Elizabeth Orthopaedic Hospital. A lunch of Devon roast beef followed at the guildhall where the Queen recalled her visit in 1946. During a fifteen-minute walkabout in the centre Prince Philip was asked to purchase a poppy but had to point out that he did not carry money. During the afternoon the royal couple toured Sowton Industrial Estate and visited B.O.C.M. Silcock Ltd, animal feed specialists. They left Exeter on a twin-engine Andover of the Queen's Flight. National newspaper coverage of the visit was dominated by Prince Philip commenting 'very handsome' on the leg of a 'shapely model' whose thigh muscles were being daubed with a felt pen at the hospital.[6]

In High Street, 9 November 1979.

Meeting Exonians on a walkabout, 9 November 1979.

The Queen receiving flowers from a child, 9 November 1979.

The Queen at the Princess Elizabeth Orthopaedic Hospital, 9 November 1979.

6

31 March 1983

Her Majesty visited Exeter once in the 1980s and hers was the first visit of a reigning queen to the cathedral. Development continued in the city: the Harlequin Centre was on the verge of being built and a stream of new buildings on the main university campus followed in the 1980s and 1990s. Weekly audiences with Mrs Thatcher had been taking place for four years. In a few months' time John Hannam would win his fifth election as Exeter's Member of Parliament.

The Queen and the Duke of Edinburgh arrived at St David's Station in the Royal Train in the morning and were received by the Earl of Morley, Lord Lieutenant, and Mayor Mrs Pat Spencer. At Broadgate they were met by Bishop Eric Mercer and the royal couple walked down the newly-built Jellicoe Steps to the West Front.

The Queen distributed Royal Maundy to 57 men and 57 women who represented each year of the sovereign's age. They were given two leather purses. The red one contained a five-pound note and a fifty pence coin while the white purse held a one penny, two pence, three pence and four pence coin.

The Duke of Edinburgh read the first lesson in the Maundy Service which was broadcast live on Radio Four. A procession through the cathedral included the sovereign's bodyguard, the Yeoman of the Guard. After a reception in the Bishop's Palace and lunch in the guildhall, there was a walkabout in the High Street. The royal couple returned to London via an aircraft of The Queen's Flight waiting at Exeter Airport.[7]

The Queen with Prince Philip and Mayor Spencer at the guildhall, 31 March 1983.

The Queen receiving flowers from a young girl, 31 March 1983.

The Queen and Prince Philip with Bishop Mercer in Cathedral Yard, 31 March 1983.

At the West Front of the cathedral, 31 March 1983.

7

19 May 1995

The Queen's next visit took place twelve years later. She was sixty-nine years old and was then receiving weekly audiences with her ninth prime minister, John Major. Three years before John Hannam had won his seventh election as the city's Member of Parliament.

The Queen and The Duke of Edinburgh arrived at ten in the morning at St David's Station in the Royal Train and were received by Major General Sir John Acland, Vice Lord Lieutenant, and Mayor Mrs Margaret Midgeley. The sun came out on their arrival. Her Majesty wore a red woollen coat and matching hat. The royal couple were driven to the University of Exeter which was celebrating its fortieth anniversary of the receipt of its Royal charter. They drove up Queen's Drive and past Queen's Building.

In the afternoon Her Majesty and His Royal Highness visited Devon County Show at Westpoint where they viewed exhibitions, presented trophies in the horse show section and afterwards had lunch. A weeping beech was planted to mark the 100th anniversary of the show. Local media coverage ('Royal Beer Run Rumpus' ran one headline) was dominated by council funds being used to transport by limousine six bottles of Double Diamond beer for Prince Philip. Meanwhile, Branscombe Vale Brewery had been given consent to name its new beer 'Royal Assent'.[8]

The Queen at the University of Exeter with Sir Geoffrey Holland, Vice Chancellor, 19 May 1995.

The Queen with Prince Philip indicating, along with the Vice Lord Lieutenant, 19 May 1995.

The Queen at the university, 19 May 1995.

The Queen planting the beech tree at the Devon County Showground, 19 May 1995.

8

27 March 1998

Her Majesty arrived in the Royal Train at St David's Station in the morning and was greeted by Lieutenant Colonel the Earl of Morley, Lord Lieutenant, and Mayor John Holman. Unusually the Duke of Edinburgh did not accompany her; he was on a tour of Bermuda. The Queen was this year having weekly audiences with her tenth prime minister, Tony Blair. Ben Bradshaw, a member of the Labour Party, had been elected Exeter's Member of Parliament the year before.

The headline in the *Express & Echo* was 'The People's Monarch!' Her Majesty crossed the river to Exwick and visited Cleve House, the South West Regional Centre of the Guide Dogs for the Blind Association. Her second visit was to St Loye's College Foundation, of which she was the patron. A short journey brought Her Majesty to the Bridge Inn in Topsham. Asked at the pub if she would like a crate of ale the Queen replied 'I'm sure the Duke might enjoy this. Will it go into the boot?' The royal couple then travelled outside Exeter's boundaries to the Commando Training Centre Royal Marines in Lympstone. A reception in the Officers' Mess was followed by lunch.

No red carpets had been laid down in Exeter and a Buckingham Palace spokesman commented 'This is not an issue. The Queen could not care less whether there is a red carpet or not, and often these days there isn't one. It is meeting local people that is important'.[9]

The Queen with the Lord Lieutenant listening to children singing at St David's Station, 27 March 1998.

The Queen at Cleve House, 27 March 1998.

The Queen watching a demonstration at St Loyes, 27 March 1998.

At the Bridge Inn, Topsham, 27 March 1998.

9

1 May 2002

The Queen, aged seventy-six, next visited Exeter four years later. Both Queen Elizabeth The Queen Mother and Princess Margaret had died months earlier. The university's Peninsula Medical School had been established in 2000 and the Met Office would relocate in 2003. Of the visit one observer wrote 'Picture the scene: little girls in glittering tiaras, little boys waving Union flags, elderly ladies sporting red, white and blue rosettes and gentlemen carrying easy-to-assemble stools'.

The visit was the start of the Golden Jubilee and the crowds became greater across the country than had been predicted. As one journalist wrote, 'if apathy and ennui were supposed to blight this tour, as a few predicted, then someone neglected to inform the West Country'. One Exeter observer noted 'the Queen's visit stopped the city in its tracks. People began lining the streets hours before her arrival. By late afternoon not a blade of grass was in evidence in Cathedral Green'.

The Queen and The Duke of Edinburgh arrived early in the evening in the Royal Train at St David's Station following a visit to Cornwall. It was later noted 'there was a great cheer as the Queen's motorcade came into view. The cheering rippled down High Street like an electric charge. A thousand flags waved frantically, a black limo came first and three police officers climbed out... The Queen was greeted by the mayor who, for a moment, looked somewhat overdressed in his splendid robes'. Lord Mayor Granville Baldwin surrendered the civic sword at the guildhall and 'Her Majesty approached the mighty sword with a friendly look in her eye, and touched the end of it with her left hand. A cheer went up and the camera flashes flickered. The Duke seemed more interested in the strange hat and picked it up off its cushion – looked askance – and then pretended to bend at the knees under the weight of it all'. The royal couple viewed the Letters Patent which had granted Lord Mayoralty to Exeter nearly 800 years after the city first had a mayor. It was estimated that 20,000 people turned out to welcome the Queen and the Duke. Afterwards, a performance took place at Exeter Cathedral and this was followed by a reception in County Hall at which the Queen spoke to farmers who had lost their herds to foot and mouth disease. She also conversed with the wives of Royal Marines who were stationed on the front line in Afghanistan.[10]

The Queen, wearing a peach and white trimmed tailored suit, pearl necklace and broach, and carrying a black handbag, on a walkabout, 1 May 2002.

The Queen, in High Street, with Eric Dancer, 1 May 2002.

Her Majesty and Prince Philip at Exeter Cathedral, 1 May 2002.

The Queen on a walkabout, 1 May 2002.

10

11 March 2010

Her Majesty came to Exeter eight years after her last visit. She was then having weekly audiences with her 11th prime minister, Gordon Brown. The Princesshay redevelopment had opened only a few years previously and the Exeter Chiefs were promoted to the Premiership in 2010.

The Queen and Prince Philip arrived in the Royal Train in the morning at St David's Station and were received by Eric Dancer, Lord Lieutenant, and Lord Mayor John Winterbottom. Her Majesty wore a purple coat and hat, black shoes and pearl earrings. The first stop was to the headquarters of St Loyes Foundation in Northernhay Place where the Queen unveiled a commemorative plaque. The royal couple then travelled to Wyvern Barracks Parade Ground where they met members of the Army Cadet Force, Air Training Corps and Sea Cadet Corps as part of the 150th anniversary of the cadet movement. Her Majesty had been Patron since 1952. The Queen and Prince Philip afterwards viewed displays and demonstrations before leaving for Dartington Hall.[11]

The Queen arriving at Northernhay Place to meet St Loyes' staff, 11 March 2010.

The Queen at Wyvern Barracks, 11 March 2010.

The Queen, escorted by Wing Commander Brian Wills-Pope, reviewing cadets at Wyvern Barracks, 11 March 2010.

Reviewing Air Cadets from 2381 (Ilminster) at Wyvern Barracks, 11 March 2010.

11

2 May 2012

Her Majesty's last visit to Exeter was part of her Diamond Jubilee tour. She was then aged eighty-six years old. Her weekly audiences were then with her 12th prime minister, David Cameron. A landmark in the commercial development of the city came in October when John Lewis opened in the refurbished former Debenham's Building. During the visit workers leaned out from the upper floors to watch the Queen's walkabout.

At 11.45 am the royal couple landed at Middlemoor where the Queen, who wore an Angela Kelly-designed deep lilac double crepe coat and matching hat, was received by Eric Dancer, Lord Lieutenant. A crowd of many thousands was in the city centre at noon, when the sun suddenly shone for the first time that day, for the walkabout in Princesshay. Amongst the well-wishers were a group of former school-children who in 1949 had witnessed Princess Elizabeth launch the rebuilding of the city with the first Princesshay. The Queen was received by Lord Mayor Stella Brock and other dignitaries included Member of Parliament Ben Bradshaw. Exeter College students performed 'Don't sit under the apple tree' and other music was provided by the Exeter Cathedral School Choir and the band of the Royal Marines.

Afterwards, the Queen visited the university and officially opened the Forum, the focal point of an extensive redevelopment of the Streatham Campus. Among the dignitaries were H. H. Dr Sheikh Sultan bin Mohammed Al Qasimi, Ruler of Sharjah. Once again there were student performances and lunch showcased local produce.

One observer wrote 'if the Queen has one powerful secret weapon no other person can have – it is that old-fashioned thing called dignity'. This journalist concluded that no other head of state matched the Queen's visibility and wrote 'maybe that won't get us far in the long-term economic run of things – perhaps it will disappear altogether when the inevitable day arrives when we no longer have her as Queen – but she is here now and I, for one, as a describer of Royal visits, enjoy witnessing the almost mystical pleasure and pride she brings to so many'.[12]

The Queen, wearing a lilac jacket and matching hat, at a walkabout in Exeter, 2 May 2012.

The Queen, with the Lord Lieutenant, meeting local dignitaries including Lord Mayor Stella Brock, 2 May 2012.

The expectant crowd at the arrival of the royal couple, 2 May 2012.

The Queen with Baroness Floella Benjamin, Chancellor, 2 May 2012.

Jubilant children in Exeter, 2 May 2012.

Epilogue

The news of the Queen's death on the 8th of September rapidly reached Exeter, like the rest of the country, through the media. The accession proclamation for King Charles III was read by the Lord Mayor at the West Front of Exeter Cathedral on the 11th, a memorial service for the Queen was held at the cathedral seven days later and there was live streaming in Northernhay Garden of the funeral. Just as the Queen's coronation had been the most publicly accessible Royal event, so too was her funeral.

Condolence books were opened at Devon County Hall, Exeter Cathedral, the Guildhall and the Royal Albert Memorial Museum. Councillor Yolonda Henson, in her capacity as Lord Mayor, visited rest homes, Royal Devon & Exeter Hospital and HM Prison Exeter for comments and signatures. These Exonians consistently expressed similar sentiments of appreciation such as 'a shining example of duty and service' and 'thank you for your unwavering service'. In Exeter there was a palpable sense of shock and grief in losing the only monarch many of us had ever known and it was also recognised, as it had been in 1903, that we would not again know another reigning queen let alone such an exceptional one.

Notes

1   *The Tatler*, 26 Nov. 1947.

2   *Western Morning News*, 13, 14 & 15 Nov. 1946; *Western Times*, 15 Nov. 1946; Tony Lethbridge, *Exeter's Royal Visitors* (Exeter, 1991), p75; *The Daily Telegraph*, 15 Nov. 1946; *The Sphere*, 23 Nov. 1946.

3   *Bradford Observer*, 22 Oct. 1949; *Western Daily Press*, 22 Oct. 1949; *Western Morning News*, 22 Oct. 1949; Lethbridge, *Royal*, pp75-7.

4   *Edinburgh Evening News*, 8 May 1956; *The Times*, 9 May 1956; *The Telegraph*, 9 May 1956; Lethbridge, *Royal*, pp77-81; *Lancashire Evening Post*, 8 May 1956; *Bradford Observer*, 10 May 1956.

5   *Express & Echo*, 5 August 1977.

6   *Torbay Express*, 9 Nov. 1979; *Express & Echo*, 9 Nov. 1979; *The Daily Telegraph*, 10 Nov. 1979.

7   *The Times*, 2 April 1983; *The Daily Telegraph*, 2 April 1983; Lethbridge, *Royal*, p84.

8   *The Daily Telegraph*, 20 May 1995; *Express & Echo*, 19 May 1995.

9   *Express & Echo*, 28 March 1998.

10   *The Daily Mail*, 2 May 2002; *The Daily Telegraph*, 2 May 2002; *Daily Post*, 2 May 2002; *Western Morning News*, 2-3 May 2002; *Express & Echo*, 2 May 2002.

11   *The Daily Telegraph*, 12 March 2010; *Express & Echo*, 12 March 2010.

12   *European Union News*, 2 May 2012; *Express & Echo*, 3 May 2012; *Western Morning News*, 3 May 2012; *Emirates News Agency*, 2 May 2012; *The Queen in the Westcountry* (*Western Morning News*, 2012).